Baptized into Christ's Death and Resurrection

Preparing to Celebrate a Christian Funeral

Volume 1: Adults

Mark G. Boyer

A Liturgical Press Book

THE LITURGICAL PRESS
Collegeville, Minnesota

Cover design and photo by Greg Becker.

1   2   3   4   5   6   7   8   9

Library of Congress Cataloging-in-Publication Data

Boyer, Mark G.
    Baptized into Christ's death and resurrection : preparing to celebrate a Christian funeral / Mark G. Boyer.
        p. cm.
    Includes index.
    Contents: v. 1. Adults — v. 2. Children.
    ISBN 0-8146-2544-4 (v. 1 : alk. paper). — ISBN 0-8146-2545-2 (v. 2 : alk. paper)
      1. Funeral service—Catholic Church—Liturgy. 2. Death—Religious aspects—Catholic Church. I. Title.
BX2035.6.F853B69   1999 v.1
264'.020985—dc21
                                     98-51062
                                          CIP

The people of long ago are not remembered,
   nor will there be any remembrance
of people yet to come
   by those who come after them.

For everything there is a season,
and a time for every matter under heaven:
   a time to be born, and a time to die. . . .

. . . [T]he fate of humans and the fate of animals is the same; as one dies, so dies the other. They all have the same breath, and humans have no advantage over the animals; for all is vanity. All go to one place; all are from the dust, and all turn to dust again.

—Eccl 1:11; 3:1-2a, 19-20

Dedicated to those members of my family
whose deaths have taught me the meaning of dying:

Sarah Osia

Charles & Meade Boyer

Jeffrey Allen Boyer

Ernest J. & Margaret M. Boyer

Jesse L. & Verna M. Boyer

Mary Ann Ackerson

Contents

Introduction

In his letter to the Romans, Paul asks, "Do you not know that all of us who have been baptized into Christ Jesus were baptized into his death?" (6:3). Then, he states, ". . . We have been buried with him by baptism into death, so that, just as Christ was raised from the dead by the glory of the Father, so we too might walk in newness of life" (6:4). The point, states the apostle, is this: "If we have been united with him in a death like his, we will certainly be united with him in a resurrection like his" (6:5).

The title for this book, *Baptized into Christ's Death and Resurrection*, comes from Paul's understanding of baptism as an immersion into the death and resurrection of Jesus Christ. The subtitle, *Preparing to Celebrate a Christian Funeral*, indicates that this book serves as a guide through the *Order of Christian Funerals*, promulgated for use in the United States on November 2, 1989. This is volume 1, a guide for funerals for adults. Volume 2 serves as a guide from the *Order of Christian Funerals* for children, both those baptized and those not baptized.

Because of many deaths in my family, not to mention the many funeral liturgies which I have celebrated for people in various parishes, I have been very much involved with death throughout my life. I have read the works of Dr. Elisabeth Kübler-Ross and taught courses to high school students and adults on dying and death. Kübler-Ross' ground-breaking work got us talking about death. Her stages of dying made us realize that the living go through the same stages after a loved one or friend has died.

Stages of Dying

In her book *On Death and Dying*, Kübler-Ross lists five stages of dying. We will review them briefly here in order to enhance our reflections and raise our awareness as we read the Scripture passages and reflections and think about the questions and journal entries in this book.

1. *Denial.* "No, not me," is what dying people say. This is a typical reaction when patients learn that they are terminally ill.

2. *Rage and Anger.* Patients ask, "Why me?" They resent the fact that others remain healthy and alive while they are dying. God can become a target for anger since God is perceived as imposing the sentence of death. God can take it, but it may be difficult for family and friends to cope with the rage and anger of the terminally ill.

3. *Bargaining.* At this stage the dying say, "Yes, me, but. . . ." They attempt to bargain with God for more time. They may bargain with others, asking them to bargain with God for more time for their loved one. The dying seem to become religious at this stage. Even those who have never prayed before seem to enter into prayer now.

4. *Depression.* Kübler-Ross says that at this point the terminally ill say, "Yes, me." They mourn past losses, things not done, wrongs committed and begin grieving and getting ready to die. As they grow quiet, they do not want visitors. Finishing their unfinished business, such as a will, disclosing the hiding place of money, being sure that a dependent person will be cared for, is the task at hand. The dying are getting ready to let go.

5. *Acceptance.* At this stage people are devoid of feeling. They say, "My time is very close now, and it is all right." They accept the reality of death and come to believe that it will not be their defeat, but their victory.

Knowing the stages of dying that Kübler-Ross has provided can help us understand what a dying loved one is going through and can aid us in helping the family member or friend in achieving the type of death wanted.

As mentioned above, the living go through the same stages, once the loved one has died. Simply stated, the living engage in denial, refusing to believe that a loved one is dying or has died. They become angry because either the dying process or the rituals surrounding death interrupt their daily routines. They may bargain, figure out ways to avoid becoming involved in either the process of dying or the process of final disposition. Depression may set in as the realization hits family and friends that the person really is dying or has died and that they, too, will one day die. Finally, acceptance of the death arrives. And, the living become more comfortable with the inevitability of their own death as well.

How Do We Learn to Die?

Today, we're out of sync with the natural process of death. Some people don't know how to die or how to face and deal with the death of a loved one because death is so well denied by our culture. Random violence or torture of any kind aside, we need to relearn the beauty of natural death and appreciate it. Because we have left our rural backgrounds and become an urban society, we no longer watch the pig being butchered or the cow being slaughtered or the chickens being killed. In a rural culture, we learned about death by watching animals die. We understood that animals die that we might live. Today, because all meat is prepared in slaughter houses, we never see the death of animals. We never feel it, smell it, taste it. Intellectually, we know that pork, beef, and chicken do not grow on a plastic plate with a cellophane wrapper, but, nevertheless, we are far removed from the reality of death. Furthermore, because few people make gardens and raise their own vegetables, we are out of tune with the way fruits and vegetables grow and give their lives to sustain ours.

Because we prefer silk flowers to real ones, which need water, trimming, and make a mess, we don't see the blossoms fade, the petals fall, and the buds drop their heads in death. Silk flowers do not die, but real ones do. We are out of touch with the reality of death when we are surrounded by silk flowers and plastic vines.

People go away to die. When people become sick and near death, they are solemnly taken away from their homes by an ambulance to a hospital, where monitors beep about life and tubes suck out one's last breath. In their older years, many people find themselves in nursing homes, waiting rooms for death. While a few relatives and friends may visit the dying in the hospital or nursing home, they never really witness death or live with it. They only visit it.

Once the dying is dead, the funeral director whisks away the body and prepares it with make-up and color and eye glasses in a fresh dress or suit. The dead look like the living. Once again, death is denied, removed. For some people, it no longer exists.

We must die from something. In the past, people simply died. If they were old, they died of old age. Now, there must be a medical reason: heart failure, lung disease, cancer. We have entered into a stage of pretend. If we can keep the heart healthy, the lungs functioning, and cancer at bay, we can live forever. That, of course, is not true. No matter how long we live, one day we will die—regardless if it is from disease or "natural causes"!

Because of our death-denying culture, it should come as no surprise that we are shocked at the death of a relative or a friend. Even if a person was elderly or had a history of heart disease or lung disease or was diagnosed with cancer and given days to live, the living are still overpowered by death's unexpectedness and their feeling of helplessness. The suddenness of the death of a younger person caused by an accident, random violence, or torture adds even more helplessness to the already-weighed down anchor of our death-denying society.

Death shocks us, rocks us from within, and grates at our thoughts because we are so far removed from it. We've forgotten or totally ignored old death and the fact that dying is a part of living. Just as we grow up learning how to live, we must also grow up learning the process of natural death. Death is certain. It brings disruption and chaos to life.

Death's Initiation Rituals

When faced with death, we want to restore order to our world. And because we live in such a fast-paced society, we want the chaos to be fixed immediately. We are one person less. For the order to return, we revert to our initiation rituals, which employ the element of water. Simultaneously we send the dead to a new world where we believe they are born again and we take our leave, saying, "Good-bye."

The rituals surrounding death are similar to those encompassing birth and baptism. Before we were born, our mother's water broke. That messy event served as a herald of our imminent arrival. On the day we were baptized, water was either poured over us or we were plunged into the font and raised up in a new birth. It is no wonder that the baptismal font is called the womb of the Church! When we die, not only does water flow out of our bodies because muscles controlling bladders no longer work, but we are sprinkled with water as a reminder that we have crossed another boundary and entered into life on the other side of the grave.

After we were born and cleaned, we were wrapped in a white blanket and solemnly presented to our parents. After we were baptized, we were dressed in a white garment and told to wear it proudly and keep it unstained until we brought it to the reign of God. For our funeral liturgy, our coffin will be clothed in a white pall, a remembrance of our baptismal garment, which has been worn on our journey to God's throne.

Our first birth was from our mother's womb. Our baptismal birth was from the womb of the Church. Our last birth is into eternal life.

When we die, we are placed in a womb-like coffin and most likely buried in mother earth. Like a dormant seed, we await the day of resurrection.

When we were born, our birth was announced with a birth certificate and cards to family and friends. When we were baptized, the minister declared our arrival with a baptismal certificate. It should come as no surprise that our last birth, death, comes with a certificate. We will have arrived at the state of new, indescribable life.

What is old decays, dissolves, disintegrates, returns to dust. Every year on Ash Wednesday, we are reminded of that fact of life: "Remember, you are dust and to dust you will return." When we are buried, the living are told, "Ashes to ashes, dust to dust." The old must be buried in order to liberate the new. Birth into eternal life cannot happen unless it is preceded by death.

The rituals surrounding a Christian funeral are those of initiation. They give us a way of confronting the chaos of death and dealing with its reality. Like an army conquering an enemy, we surround death, kill it, and pull order and life out of it by using our rituals. The dead cross over the waters of chaos to the promised land on the other side.

What we may have failed to recognize is that we are doing this throughout our lives. We're always being re-initiated into the depths of life—of course, only after we die! In other words, every chaos we face and enter plunges us into darkness where we battle death and emerge, paradoxically, diminished but enriched. We are fuller of life and fuller of death. We have experienced being raised from the dead to new life.

Frequently, this experience occurs in relationships—friendships or marital unions. Disagreement breeds words that sting. Both parties in the relationship have to take responsibility for the problem and the solution. That means that both die in order that both can rise to a new life as friends or husband and wife.

Employers can be so removed from their employees that they lose touch with the work their employees actually do on a daily basis. When an employee approaches the boss and offers a more efficient method for accomplishing the daily tasks, if both are willing to dialogue, enter into a mutual conversation of understanding, giving and taking, they die and rise to new life for the company.

We experience death and resurrection when making a transition from one state in life to another, such as from high school to college or from college to the work force or from single life to married life. We make choices, dying to several career possibilities in order to have one, dying to many friends of the opposite sex in order to have one in marriage. With every change there comes some death to the previous way of life. However, as one enters into this new way of life, more life begins to emerge and flow. The dynamic of death and life continue throughout our lives—until we take our last breath.

Letting go is an important part of living because it enables us to practice dying. If we've died throughout our lives, then final death will not have all the fears our culture seems to associate with it. The gospel-perspective is that of entrusting ourselves into the hands of God, like Jesus, who said that he would do his Father's will—no matter how difficult it would be or how much of it he did not know or understand.

Accepting our own mortality, which we make great efforts to cover up, enables us to live well. Living well is learning how to die well. Instead of hiding our dust with make-up and hair and beard coloring, tummy tucks and liposuction, body-building, amassing things and money to keep alive the illusion that we will conquer death, we live healthier lives by letting go. As we let go, we learn the great truth that less is more.

Technology, while it is good and can help us lead healthier lives, can lead us to believe that we will live forever. Kidney dialysis, by-pass heart surgery, spare-part-organ replacement surgery, and other medical procedures mean that we can squeeze a few more years out of the old, tired body. Non-fat or low-fat foods, skim milk, no-cholesterol diets offer us more years of life. Doctors can become modern exorcists, technicians who ward off death with pills and shots, tubes and surgery. Ordinary food can become the eucharist that sustains us in this life. And still death remains inevitable!

The lot, the end, of every human being is death. Sooner or later death comes to get us, whether we are ready or not. We can try to ensure that our names will be remembered once we are dead, but that is futile. We cannot do a thing about remembrance once we are no longer here and cannot remember anyway.

Living the dynamic of death and life in the spirit is where real life is found. Dying and being reborn is the fullness of living. We can be reborn to a depth of life that we cannot imagine, let alone attempt to describe.

View of Life Influences View of Death

There are at least three images we use to think about life. Each of these influences the way we think about death. Most people think that life is linear. We enter the time-line of the world at a certain point and leave it at a certain point. Like an arrow, we travel throughout our lives until we hit the bull's eye. We're born, grow up, marry, age, die. The arrow hits the target, never to return to the archer. Pilgrims complete their journeys. Throughout the years of our lives, we experience living but we are always looking back to what has been and forward to what will be. Like a river, life is flowing. We can fail to live in the present. For those who view life as a linear time-line, death is the end of our years. Like the hypochondriac in a cartoon said, "Death runs in my family."

Life can be viewed as circular. We are born, grow up, marry, age, and die. Then, someone else is born, grows up, marries, ages, and dies. And it goes on and on, like the seasons, which continue to repeat themselves: spring, summer, fall, winter, spring, summer, fall, winter. Such a circular view of living is like recycling. Every death is replaced with a new birth. In this understanding death is the end of one person's circle and the beginning of another's. Life and death just keep going on, circling.

Lastly, life can be viewed as a spiral. This is a combination of the linear and circular views. Life goes around and around, but it is going somewhere. With every experience of living, we delve deeper into the intimate dynamic of life and death and we move upward and outward into the dynamic of life and death. Simultaneously, we are enriched and diminished. In this third view, we keep growing until we discover God in the depths of our being and the universe in its limitless expanse. We discover that we are one, united with all that is in both its smallness and its greatness. Final death becomes a new experience for which we anxiously await because it will plunge us even more into the mystery of life.

Faith and Death

"It is in regard to death that [our] condition is most shrouded in doubt," states Vatican Council II's December 7, 1965, Pastoral Constitution on the Church in the Modern World (par. 18). We are "tormented not only by pain and by the gradual breaking-up of [the] body but also, and even more, by the dread of forever ceasing to be" (par. 18). However, there is "a deep instinct" within us that leads us "rightly to shrink from and to reject the utter ruin and total loss of . . . personality" (par. 18). We bear in ourselves the seed of eternity which cannot be reduced simply to matter, and so we rebel against death. We come to understand that modern technology can prolong life, "but this does not satisfy . . . heartfelt longing, one that can never be stifled, for a life to come" (par. 18).

The Pastoral Constitution on the Church in the Modern World addresses how belief in God and faith in a life hereafter provide a sense of meaning and impose a semblance of order in a world and existence otherwise undermined by death. It says, "While the mind is at a loss before the mystery of death, the Church, taught by divine Revelation, declares that God has created [people] in view of a blessed destiny that lies beyond the limits of [this] sad state on earth. Moreover, the Christian faith teaches that bodily death . . . will be overcome when that wholeness which [was] lost [through sin] . . . will be given once again . . . by the almighty and merciful Savior" (par. 18).

God has called us and still calls us to cleave with all our being to God "in sharing for ever a life that is divine and free from all decay" (par. 18). The Constitution continues, "Christ won this victory when he rose to life, for by his death he freed [us] from death. Faith, therefore, with its solidly based teaching, provides every thoughtful [person] with an answer to [the] anxious queries about his [or her] future lot" (par. 18). We who have been made partners with Christ in the paschal mystery and who have been configured to his death can die in faith that God will raise us to new life, just like God raised Christ.

Instead of picturing death as coming to destroy us, faith enables us to picture Christ as saving us. Instead of seeing death as an end, faith helps us see death as a new beginning with more abundant life. Life is changed; it is not ended. Death is not a loss says faith, but a gain; not a parting, but a meeting; not a going away, but an arrival. Life on the other side of the grave is as much a mystery as life on this side! We are more than we can conceive of ourselves to be! Life is a being-toward death; death is a being-toward life!

The Pastoral Constitution on the Church in the Modern World extends the offer of life after death to all people: ". . . this holds true not for Christians only but also for all . . . of good will in whose hearts grace is active invisibly. For since Christ died for all, and since all . . . are in fact called to one and the same destiny, which is divine, we must hold that the Holy Spirit offers to all the possibility of being made partners, in a way known to God, in the paschal mystery" (par. 22).

Who Should Use This Book?
When Should This Book Be Used?

This book is meant to be used primarily in preparation for celebrating the rites found in the *Order of Christian Funerals* at the time of the death of an adult loved one. It can be used by members of the family to select rites and Scripture passages which best express the life of the deceased and the circumstances of death, to help meet the spiritual and psychological needs of the family and friends of the deceased to express grief and loss, to support the living as they accept the reality of death and comfort one another, and to proclaim the paschal mystery in which all share: death and resurrection.

This book can be used by those who desire to plan their own funeral rites. The last chapter provides forms upon which you can indicate Scripture passages and music which you may want to be used in your vigil service, funeral liturgy, committal, and Office for the Dead.

Bishops, priests, deacons, and anyone who ministers to the family and friends of the dead person at the time of a funeral will find the reflections in this book helpful, especially in conjunction with celebrating the various rites in the *Order of Christian Funerals*. The reflections form a resource which can be used for homilies or sermons and instruction based on the Word of God. The forms in the last chapter can serve as a guide in preparing the various rites and keeping a record of selections made by the family of the deceased.

Anyone needing a guide for some thoughts about death can use this book in the fall, especially those days surrounding the annual celebration of All Souls Day, November 2. As the earth sheds her outer garments in death, we hold onto the life that will burst forth once winter has passed. The interplay of death and resurrection during fall and spring provides an opportunity to reflect on death, using this book.

Lent, that season of dust and ashes, is a good time to think about death. Not only do we recall the death of the Lord, but we think about our own. This book can serve as a guide for the reader throughout the entire Season of Lent.

Because Lent focuses on two aspects of the paschal mystery—suffering and death—and Easter on the resurrection, this book can be used as a guide throughout the Easter Season, too. Often it refers to the paschal mystery and the hope that all people share in new life beyond the grave.

Adult discussion groups will find this book a source for much dialogue. Members of such groups can read specific parts of the book and share their answers with each other to the questions for reflection and the journal exercises.

Since the book is a resource, there is no limit to the ways in which it can be used as a spiritual tool in preparing to celebrate the rites of the *Order of Christian Funerals*.

The Six-Part Process

The Scriptures employed in the celebration of each rite of the *Order of Christian Funerals* are the basis for this work. The six-part process stems from and is grounded in the Word of God.

First, the notations for the texts from Scripture are given along with selections from Scripture for each rite of the *Order of Christian Funerals*. From the funeral rites for adults selections are made from each of the Scripture passages in Parts I (Sections 1-6), III (Sections 13 and 16), and IV (Sections 17 and 18) of the *Order of Christian Funerals*, including the psalms. This book follows the order of the rites in the *Order of Christian Funerals* for adults, maintaining the section numbers of the *Order*, cross-referencing Scripture passages when they are used in more than one rite, and maintaining the language used in the *Order*.

Second, a reference from the English translation of the *Order of Christian Funerals* has been selected to complement the Scripture choice or develop a deeper understanding of it. The instructive material in the *Order* is a source for reflection, meditation, and guidance. Those desiring to read the paragraph references to the *Order* can find them in either *Order of Christian Funerals: General Introduction and Pastoral Notes: Liturgy Documentary Series 8* (Washington, D.C.: Office for Publishing and Promotion Services, United States Catholic Conference, 1989) or *Order of Christian Funerals* (Collegeville, Minn.: The Liturgical Press, 1989).

A reflection forms the third part of the process. The reflection presents ideas about how we might approach the Scripture passage and the reference from the *Order of Christian Funerals*. The reflection develops key themes, images, and words found in the Scripture selection and the provided reference.

Some of the reflections are general and, if used in preaching a homily, will have to be tailored to the specific vigil or funeral liturgy. We cannot be specific about what is on the other side of death, since we cannot know what's "over there." We believe that what God did for Jesus—raise him from the dead—God will do for us. The beginning and end of every reflection is faith in Christ's resurrection from the dead.

The fourth part, the questions for reflection, consists of questions which ask readers to think about a recent experience of their life and identify how God was present and active in their life. The questions are for thinking, although that does not exclude the possibility of recording some of one's thoughts. The point of the questions for reflection, which should take 10 to 15 minutes, is to see

God's activity in the more recent, ordinary events of life and
death.

The fifth part of the process is a prayer. It summarizes the ideas,
themes, and images in the Scripture passage and the quotation from
the *Order of Christian Funerals* developed in the reflection and upon
which one reflected using the questions provided. The prayers are
personal. They praise God for gifts and calls in the past and petition for similar gifts and calls in the present and future.

Finally, a journal exercise is provided. This activity is meant
to be written in a notebook or journal. The exercise asks readers to
review some major events and experiences of life and death in their
lives and to pinpoint how God has been leading and guiding them.
It asks readers to journey backward and to mine the rich veins of
their experiences of God.

The journal exercise flows out of the reflection and the questions for reflection. It builds on and is designed to expand the reader's
personal reflections. Our future is conditioned by our past. Often
we are warmed by fires we did not build and we drink from wells
we did not dig. By examining those fires and wells, we raise our con-
sciousness of God's activity in our lives in the past, no matter if we
were aware of it at that time or not. This part of the exercise will
take 15 to 30 minutes.

It is the author's hope that the reader will grow in the spirit-
uality of the paschal mystery—the death and resurrection of Jesus
Christ—and grow in life through death, being continually formed
into the likeness of Christ by the Holy Spirit, a likeness begun in
the waters of baptism, repeated through life, and celebrated in the
rites surrounding death.

PART I

Funeral Rites

Part I of the *Order of Christian Funerals* is divided into three groups of rites that correspond in general to the three principal ritual moments in the funerals of Christians: "Vigil and Related Rites and Prayers," "Funeral Liturgy," and "Rite of Committal."

—*Order of Christian Funerals,* par. 50.

Vigil
and Related Rites and Prayers

Order of Christian Funerals: par. 52.

1. Vigil for the Deceased

Order of Christian Funerals: par. 56.

Vigil for the Deceased

FIRST READING: BODY-TENT

Scripture: (2 Cor 5:1, 6-10) . . . [W]e know that if the earthly tent we live in is destroyed, we have a building from God, a house not made with hands, eternal in the heavens. . . . So we are always confident; even though we know that while we are at home in the body we are away from the Lord—for we walk by faith, not by sight (5:1, 6-7).

Order of Christian Funerals: par. 7.

Reflection: Most of us have seen a tent. It may have been pitched as a shelter for a booth during a parish picnic. Maybe the tent we saw was set up to enclose a space for the circus.

In cemeteries a tent is usually erected over the grave where a person is to be buried. When people go backpacking and camping in the mountains, usually they take a tent along with them to serve as their bedroom for the night.

A tent is a collapsible shelter, made of canvas or some water-resistant fabric stretched over wooden or aluminum poles. A tent is a temporary shelter from the sun, the rain, the snow, and the wind. It is not like a house, which is permanent and built to last for years. A tent is pitched for only a night or a few days, and then it is taken down.

Our bodies are tents for our earthly dwelling, our earthly existence. We use our bodies to express who we are from the depths of our hidden persons, from the secret places of our hearts. All that we see, taste, hear, smell, and touch enters into us through our body-tent. We can either open up our body-tent flaps to let others into our lives or we can close them and keep others out.

2

We know that we are more than our bodies. There is more to us than what we see as an outside tent-covering. That "moreness"—call it personality or soul—is nothing other than the mystery of God within us. This body is the tent that God gives us as a covering, a means of protection, and a vehicle for expressing the mystery of the invisible God within us who becomes incarnate in our flesh.

Like a physical tent, we are always moving our body-tents, taking them from one place to another in order to share with others the God we enclose within them. So, we are not completely at home here on earth in our temporary dwelling. Our real home is a building from God, a dwelling not made with hands, eternal in heaven. God gives us this temporary body-tent to live in until we go home to the Lord.

Death is the folding up of our earthly dwelling, our body-tent. Our body-tent is not permanent, although at times we may pretend it is. No matter how hard we try to make it permanent—and with all the modern technology we have, some of us get pretty good at trying—one day our pilgrimage will end and our tent will be destroyed.

The end of this tent is as certain and inevitable and real as streaks of summer lightning, or a flash flood, or the earth beneath our feet. We cannot bribe death by giving it a thousand dollars and telling it to get lost. We cannot put it off and say, "Come back next week and I'll decide if I am ready; let me think about it for a few days."

In one of her famous poems Emily Dickinson captured the inevitability of death when she wrote, "Because I could not stop for Death, / He kindly stopped for me. . . ." Our temporary body-tents are, well, just that—temporary.

When a person dies, his or her death reminds us of our temporary, merely-passing-through, tent-status. We gather to honor the person's body-tent, which, in the words of Jesuit Father Gerard Manley Hopkins, flamed out the incarnate presence of God "like shining from shook foil."

We are reminded of our own mortality. We are like the seriously ill John Donne, who one day heard the church bells tolling the death of someone and wrote, ". . . [N]ever send to know for whom the bell tolls; it tolls for thee."

The death of anyone reminds us of our own inevitable future. One day each one of us will be waked and "funeraled" and buried, once we have closed the eyes of our earthly tent in death.

However, death, the dismantling of this body-tent, is not the end. Death is not a period, but a comma in the sentence of life. We profess our faith that death is not the end. Life is changed, not ended. When the body of our earthly tent lies in death, we gain an everlasting place in heaven.

Maybe Anna, the famous child-prodigy from the book *Mister God, This Is Anna,* said it best in *Anna's Book* as told by her friend, Fynn: "Anna concluded that when a thing changed its shape it was because it had something else to do for Mister God. For Anna, death was just one of those things that happened. Death was that point in life when you began to change shape."

Questions for Reflection: In what ways do you walk by faith and not by sight? In what ways do you live as though your body-tent were permanent? What reminds you of the temporary status of your body-tent?

Prayer: God of eternal life, you give to me a temporary earthly tent to dwell in so that you might lead me to your heavenly dwelling place. Guide my steps in the way of faith. Calm my fears with your mercy. Awaken in me the hope of the resurrection that I may one day see you as you are: eternal Trinity—Father, Son, and Holy Spirit for ever. Amen.

Journal: Make a list of what you fear about death, the taking down of your body-tent. Identify how your hope for eternal life can calm each of your fears.

RESPONSORIAL PSALM: PS 27

See Part III: Texts of Sacred Scripture—13. Funerals for Adults, Responsorial Psalms, 3. Expression of Trust.

GOSPEL: WAITING FOR THE MASTER

Scripture: (Luke 12:35-40) [Jesus said,] "Be dressed for action and have your lamps lit; be like those who are waiting for their master to return from the wedding banquet, so that they may open the door for him as soon as he comes and knocks. . . . If he comes during the middle of the night, or near dawn, and finds them so, blessed are those slaves" (12:35-36, 38).

Order of Christian Funerals: par. 1.

Reflection: We spend a lot of time waiting. We wait in a line in the supermarket to have the total cost of our cart of groceries added up so that we can pay for them and go home. We wait in line at the airport to check in, to get a boarding pass, to go to the waiting area so that we can wait some more. We wait for trains and buses, at traffic lights, for help in department stores. In the doctor's office or dentist's office we await our turn to have our bodies examined or our teeth cleaned. Is death just one more event for which we wait? Yes and No.

Yes, each person awaits—either calmly or anxiously—the day of his or her death. Death is inevitable. It is an inescapable aspect of being human. One day—near or far—every one of us will face the end. The heart will stop pumping, the lungs will cease breathing, brain waves will no longer be detectable. We will be dead, and our wait will have come to an end.

No, death is not just one more event for which we wait. For those who believe that God has created us for eternal life, death is but another stage of growth. Just as we progress from being an infant to a child, to a teenager, to an adult, to middle age, to the more mature years, to old age, so do we progress from old age through death to new life. The light of faith of our body-lamp does not go out. We servants are always dressed and ready for the master to come home and invite us to the next stage of growth—eternal life.

Our body-lamps burn with the oil of good deeds, with the kind words we have spoken to others, with the genuine care we have shown to all our brothers and sisters, and with all the times that we have accepted the suffering in our lives that helped to mold us into the image of Jesus, whom God raised from the dead. As O. Henry, the famous short-story writer, said when he was dying, "Turn up the lights—I don't want to go home in the dark." Our lamp of faith burns brightly so that we don't go home in the dark.

Keeping plenty of oil in our lamps is how we are prepared for the master to come home. He may arrive during the middle of the night while we sleep. He will ask, "Ready?" Seeing the lamp burning, we will be able to respond, "Ready!" He may come near the dawn, in the early morning, as the first streaks of the new day are etched upon the eastern sky. He will ask, "Are you prepared?" And we, seeing the light, will say, "Let's go!" No matter when he comes, if he finds our lamps burning, he will call us "blessed." The master will congratulate us and lead us over the border of death to the new land of eternal life.

Questions for Reflection: Identify the oil in your lamp that keeps it burning. Is death just another event for which you wait, or do you see it as another state of growth? Explain.

Prayer: God, my master, through the waters of baptism you clothed me for action and instructed me to wait for the coming of your Son, Jesus Christ, whom you raised from the dead. Help me to be a good servant, filling my lamp with the oil of goodness. Make me ready for death. I ask this through Christ the risen Lord. Amen.

Journal: How do you envision the master coming home? If you were able to plan your own death, what would it look like?

Vigil for the Deceased with Reception at the Church

Order of Christian Funerals: par. 54.

FIRST READING: CHILDREN OF GOD

Scripture: (1 John 3:1-2) See what love the Father has given us, that we should be called children of God; and that is what we are. . . . Beloved, we are God's children now; what we will be has not yet been revealed (3:1a, 2a).

Order of Christian Funerals: par. 5.

Reflection: I don't like being treated like a child, and I don't like being called a child. I think of myself as an adult, a person who is capable of thinking through problems, reaching moral, rational decisions, and implementing them in my life. So, when someone shakes a finger at me in warning or takes me to task for having made a mistake, I respond with anger at being treated like a child. When I hear, "Even a kid wouldn't have done this," I know that I am being called a child. I prefer to live in the world of adults.

However, when it comes to God, all of us are children. God calls us children because in God's eyes we can never grow up. In our earthly life, children sooner or later enter a plain where they are considered equal to, if not greater than, their parents. They enter into the adult world of work, finance, marriage, child-rearing. They grow up—physically, psychologically, emotionally, and spiritually. Once we pass through death to new life, we do not know what the world of adults looks like. Such reality has not yet been revealed to us.

The funeral of a loved one or a friend becomes our opportunity to profess our faith as children in the hope of whatever God has planned for us as adults on the other side of the grave. We simultaneously praise God for the gift of the life of the deceased "child," which has returned to the Creator, and we place our hope in the Father, who has not shown us what exists on the other side of death.

We can be sure of this: No parent would consciously lead a child down the wrong path. God, who calls us children, is worthy of trust, no matter what the mystery, even the "adulthood" on the other side of death.

Questions for Reflection: In what ways do you act like a child of God? How do you think the adult world in which you live now influences your understanding of what you will be one day on the other side of death?

Prayer: Unseen God, as a Father you bring me to birth and guide my steps throughout my life. I worship and praise and thank you for such a wonderful gift as life. Help me to keep in mind that I am your child, as I await the revelation of what you will one day make me after death. Give me hope through Jesus Christ, your Son, who lives and reigns with you and the Holy Spirit, one God, for ever and ever. Amen.

Journal: What do you think "adulthood" with God will be like? What aspect of "adulthood" with God is most fearsome to you? Explain.

RESPONSORIAL PSALM: PS 103

See Part III: Texts of Sacred Scripture—13. Funerals for Adults, Responsorial Psalms, 6. Reconciliation.

GOSPEL: MANY HOUSES

Scripture: (John 14:1-6) [Jesus said,] "In my Father's house there are many dwelling places. If it were not so, would I have told you that I go to prepare a place for you? And if I go and prepare a place for you, I will come again and will take you to myself, so that where I am, there you may be also" (14:2-3).

Order of Christian Funerals: par. 8.

Reflection: Most of us have seen an apartment or, maybe, lived in one. An apartment usually consists of one to three rooms inside of a building which houses many such dwellings. A main door permits those who live in the apartment building to share a common entrance to the building, while dwellers have separate doors which admit them to their apartments. In many cases, apartment buildings are constructed together and form apartment complexes. Hundreds of people can share the same basic building but live in their own individual spaces.

In John's Gospel, Jesus speaks about heaven, using the metaphor of an apartment to talk about what is on the other side of the grave. God is the owner of the heavenly apartment complex consisting of an infinite number of individual dwellings, enough for all people. Each apartment has been prepared by God's Son, Jesus

Christ, but people of all races and languages and ways of life and religions will live in them. He has covered the dirty walls of sin with the fresh paint of mercy. He has replaced the curtained windows of despair with uncovered panes of hope. With the promise of eternal life, Jesus has refurnished every room.

Once God's Son finished redecorating every apartment through his own death and resurrection, he not only promised those who believe in him an apartment, but he assured them that he would become their escort to their individual dwelling places. In other words, Jesus is the bellhop who will show us to our rooms. Thus, we will live next door to all others who believe in the name of God's Son, who have led a good life, who have done God's will, and next door to Jesus, who dwells for ever with God.

The apartment complex metaphor offers us a way to speak about the unknown by using an image of what we know. Ultimately, our hope is not for a well-furnished, heavenly apartment, but for the life beyond the grave, which Jesus already shares and promises to us.

Questions for Reflection: How do you envision your apartment in heaven? With what is it furnished? What does each item represent for you?

Prayer: Father of the eternal house, through the death and resurrection of your Son, Jesus Christ, you have prepared a dwelling place for me. Keep my eyes fixed upon it. At the end of my life, send Jesus to take me to my room so that I might share in your life for ever. I ask this through Jesus Christ the Lord. Amen.

Journal: Besides the apartment-complex image for whatever is on the other side of death, of what other metaphors can you think? Make a list and explain each metaphor.

2. Related Rites and Prayers

Order of Christian Funerals: par. 99.

Prayers After Death

Order of Christian Funerals: par. 102

READING A: PRESENCE

Scripture: (Matt 18:19-20) [Jesus said,] ". . . [I]f two of you agree on earth about anything you ask, it will be done for you by my Father in heaven. For where two or three are gathered in my name, I am there among them" (18:19-20).

Order of Christian Funerals: par. 8.

Reflection: Because there is no story of an ascension in Matthew's Gospel, Jesus is portrayed by the author as remaining with the church, the community of believers, "to the end of the age" (Matt 28:20). He is "'Emmanuel,' which means, 'God is with us'" (Matt 1:23). Therefore, whenever two or more people gather together in his name, Jesus is among them.

In the first-century church for which Matthew was writing, the community of believers was far more important than the individual believer, the exact opposite of contemporary American society. Matthew placed the church above the individual, not downgrading the person but placing Jesus' presence within the community. Whatever action the community would take, it would be what God wanted, according to Matthew's perspective.

Thus, when a person dies, the community shares in the death, because that individual was baptized into the church and shared the same table. In other words, the community, composed of those still living and the deceased, recognizes Jesus' presence in gathering in his name. In the face of death, the community continues to gather and consoles those who mourn the loss of a member. It can be said that the community in which Jesus is present has a ministry of consoling itself.

The church is like a mirror. When we look into the mirror we see our own image. However, when the church looks into the mirror, it sees the image of Jesus in the whole of its members. In the face of the reality of death, the members reflect the consolation of

Jesus to those who mourn. The members of the church mirror the eternal presence of Jesus with us. Nothing, not even death, separates the members of the church in Matthew's view. Jesus is with the community until the end of time.

Questions for Reflection: In what ways does the promise of Jesus to be with the church until the end of the age give you consolation and hope? How do you think your parish community has been a mirror of Jesus to those who mourn?

Prayer: Eternal God, you never cease to guide your church from one generation to the next with the presence of Emmanuel, Jesus, your Son. Help me to be a faithful member, recognizing the presence of Jesus Christ and offering his hope and consolation to those who mourn. I ask this in his name. Amen.

Journal: Identify the ways that you, as a member of the church, offer consolation to those who mourn. How are you a mirror reflecting the presence of Jesus to others?

READING B: PROOF OR FAITH

Scripture: (John 11:21-24) Martha said to Jesus, "Lord, if you had been here, my brother would not have died. But even now I know that God will give you whatever you ask of him." Jesus said to her, "Your brother will rise again." Martha said to him, "I know that he will rise again in the resurrection on the last day" (11:21-24).

Order of Christian Funerals: par. 9.

Reflection: There is a difference between knowing and believing. Knowledge implies certainty, insofar as it is bounded by human limitation. Believing implies trust without certainty. You can know that this book has a cover and printed text on its pages because you are reading it now. However, without having investigated it, you cannot know that. You may believe it, but your belief, after investigation, may turn out to have been in error.

In John's Gospel, Martha uses the word "knowing" as a synonym for the word "believing" to emphasize her faith. Martha believes that if Jesus had been present Lazarus would not have died. Martha believes that God will give Jesus whatever he asks. Martha believes that Lazarus will rise in the resurrection on the last day. Later in the story, the Johannine Jesus asks her point blank, Do you believe in me? And she professes her faith in him as both the Messiah and the Son of God.

Faith has no proof. If we believe only a little, we have faith. Faith, by definition, is belief in and trust in God. It is unshakable on the part of the believer even when those who do not believe attempt to prove how ridiculous faith without knowledge really is.

The story of Martha, Lazarus, Mary, and Jesus in John's Gospel is told to highlight the differences between knowledge and faith. In the community for whom the gospel was written, there were people who wanted proof that Jesus was the Messiah and the Son of God. All the evidence suggested Jesus was not the biological son of a descendent of David's line—the meaning of Messiah (Anointed, Christ)—and no one had ever heard of God, pure spirit, becoming flesh before. Added to those problems was a waning faith in the resurrection as the community watched some of its first members die.

The Johannine Jesus calls forth faith from Martha. Today, Jesus continues to call forth faith from us—faith that this life is not all there is. However, we cannot know what is on the other side of death or even prove that there is anything on the other side of death. All we can do is believe that there is life "over there," and through our faith offer comfort to those who are mourning the loss of a loved one.

Questions for Reflection: For you what is the difference between knowing and believing? Do you tend to lean toward the knowing (proof) side of the continuum or toward the believing (trust) side? Explain.

Prayer: God of life, like Jesus, your Son, acknowledged Martha's faith, you invite me to trust the mystery of your love. Give me a faith like Martha's. Strengthen my faith in Jesus, whom you raised from the dead, and in the resurrected life you have prepared for me. Hear my prayer through Christ the Lord. Amen.

Journal: How do you think living in an everything-has-to-be-proved society influences your faith? Make a list of the ways that you attempt to prove what you believe. After finishing the list, think about this question: What does your list prove?

READING C: BONDS NOT BROKEN

Scripture: (Luke 20:35-38) [Jesus said,] ". . . [T]hose who are considered worthy of a place . . . in the resurrection from the dead neither marry nor are given in marriage. Indeed they cannot die anymore, because they are like angels and are children of God, being children of the resurrection" (20:35-36).

Order of Christian Funerals: par. 4.

Reflection: Draw a line down the center of a sheet of paper. Label the line "death." To the left of the line make a list of the metaphors we use for death. To the right of the line make a list of the metaphors we use for resurrection. A metaphor, a figure of speech in which a word or phrase literally denoting one kind of object or idea is used in place of another to suggest a likeness or analogy between them, draws upon common, human experience to talk of that about which we know nothing—what is on the other side of death.

For example, we use the daily experience of sleep to speak about death. Haven't you ever heard someone during a wake say, "Aunt Mary looks like she's sleeping." To emphasize the "sleeping" dimension of the death-metaphor we place Aunt Mary on a small bed complete with a pillow and, sometimes, with an inner-spring mattress! We know that Aunt Mary is dead and not sleeping. But the common, daily experience provides the metaphor for us to talk about the resurrection by saying, "Aunt Mary will wake up." We know that Aunt Mary will not "wake up," but that is the best we can do in attempting to describe what is on the other side of death, an experience which none of us has ever had. In essence, we are saying that resurrection is like waking up from sleep every day. Death is like taking a long night's sleep, and resurrection is like being awakened and totally refreshed.

Another example of a metaphor we use for death is awaiting a second birth. Just as we were born once from our mother's womb, we will be born again from mother earth to new life. We emphasize the new-dimension of the metaphor by placing the body of the dead in some type of container, usually called a casket or coffin, supposedly resembling a uterus, and then put both into a hole dug into the side of mother earth. (It's like a reverse cesarean section!) After the necessary period of gestation, we posit that mother earth will give birth to the dead. That birth will be resurrection.

Notice that metaphors do not prove resurrection; they attempt to give a glimpse of that which is not seeable. Today, more than ever, there is a growing interest in attempting to prove the resurrection. Many people gather to hear those who have had near-death experiences tell about tunnels and light in the hope that they can prove the resurrection for their listeners. Our scientific world wants proof that there is life on the right side of the line.

However, resurrection is a mystery, meaning that an understanding of it is reserved only for God. Near-death experiences are simply that—near-death experiences. A person who is resuscitated was never dead to begin with. Resuscitation is not a good metaphor for resurrection! Once a person dies, he or she is dead. Once the line is crossed, no one returns.

The question about resurrection can preoccupy inquiring minds which seek scientific proof in the face of mystery. The intense interest in our own day concerning death and dying and near-death experiences indicates our curiosity about and fear of death (the line) and lack of faith in the resurrection (what is to the right of the line). Books, TV programs, and tapes on the market tell us that the lifelike makeup on a dead body in a coffin and the floral spray on top only cover up the finality of death. Sooner or later, we must realize that death is real and final; we are finite. Until we face the fact of our own personal death, we can pretend to be immortal. The day we confront our mortality is also the day we can begin to trust the mystery of the resurrection, nothing other than trusting God.

There are no metaphors that adequately compare the next life to this life. Resurrection is new life—not an extension of this life. God makes a new creation out of us after death. That is God's promise, which we, believers in the resurrection, are invited to trust.

Questions for Reflection: What identity do you think you will have on the other side of death? Do you think that you will be able to recognize those you have loved, such as parents, brothers and sisters, children?

Prayer: God of the resurrection, you invite me to trust that what you did for your Son, Jesus Christ, you will do for me: raise me from the dead. While I search for words to describe what life must be like on the other side of the grave, I believe that I cannot die again. When I am weak in faith, help me to profess my belief that you not only raised Jesus from the dead, but you made him Lord for ever and ever. Amen.

Journal: What do you think resurrection will be like? Will we wake up, be born again, find that our tomb is empty? What is your favorite metaphor for resurrection? Explain why.

Gathering in the Presence of the Body

Order of Christian Funerals: pars. 109, 110.

SCRIPTURE VERSE A: LAY DOWN YOUR YOKE

Scripture: (Matt 11:28-30) [Jesus said,] "Come to me, all you that are weary and are carrying heavy burdens, and I will give you rest.

Take my yoke upon you, and learn from me; for I am gentle and humble in heart, and you will find rest for your souls. For my yoke is easy, and my burden is light" (11:28-30).

Order of Christian Funerals: par. 22.

Reflection: At the end of a long day, who doesn't feel tired and weary? From dawn to sunset, countless tasks have been completed. The morning rituals, such as showering, eating breakfast, reading the newspaper, were finished. The children were sent off to school, while parents drove to work. Lunch was eaten either in or outside of the workplace. More work was done throughout the afternoon until it was time to go home, prepare dinner, take care of various household chores, such as taking out the trash, doing the laundry, dusting, getting ready for the next day, and getting everyone to bed. The heavy burdens of the day have been carried for about sixteen hours; now it is time to lay them down and get some rest.

Death represents the laying down of our lifetime yoke. From birth to death we carry the heavy burdens of living. As children we learn the discipline needed to share burdens with the other members of our families. During our teenage years, we are initiated into the weary world of peer pressure, and we struggle to find our own identity. As young adults, we venture into new relationships and, maybe, marriage. Caring for children puts another yoke on our shoulders until they are old enough to take care of themselves. During our golden years, we must redefine our lives again as we realize that most of our years have been lived and death, which could never touch us before, looms on the horizon. Finally, the older years may burden us with ill health, nursing homes, or diseases which leave us unable to care for ourselves. Death is the final release from our lifetime burdens.

Death enables us to lay down everything, including our lives, in the hope of eternal rest. Suffering and death no longer have a hold on us; we are set free as God calls us home.

Maybe one of the most fearful aspects of dying is turning ourselves loose from our lifetime yoke. After all, we spend a lifetime gathering it together and making it heavy and hard to carry. By setting it down, we disassociate ourselves from our burdens and associate ourselves with Jesus, the one who has shown us that we go to him with nothing but the hope for rest.

Questions for Reflection: What are the various elements which make up the yoke you carry? How do you identify who you are with the yoke you bear?

Prayer: Through the easy yoke and light burden of Jesus, eternal God, you have shown me rest. Help me to lay down my heavy burdens and to go and to learn from him. Strengthen me in my older years to face death with gentleness and humility that I may find rest in you alone. Hear my prayer through Christ the Lord. Amen.

Journal: What do you understand the easy yoke and gentle burden of Jesus to be? What do you think eternal rest will be like? What is the greatest difficulty you have in setting down your yoke?

SCRIPTURE VERSE B: TROUBLED?

Scripture: (John 14:1-3) [Jesus said,] "Do not let your hearts be troubled. Believe in God, believe also in me" (14:1).

Order of Christian Funerals: par. 4.

Reflection: When we are troubled, we worry and we experience mental agitation. It is difficult to let go of what bothers us. For example, we are troubled by the announcement that the company for which we work is downsizing or closing a part of its operations where we work. We worry about losing our job, our family, having to go back to school to be retrained, having to move, etc.

Special celebrations can become troubled times for some people. When a son or daughter is married, we may worry before the wedding about the wedding plans, about the cake, the reception, the compatibility of the couple. It is hard to let go of our troubles and celebrate the present moment of two people pledging their lives to each other.

Parents are often troubled by the grades their children get in high school and college. They worry about the children's friends, where they go, how late they stay out. Spiritual agitation comes upon parents as they discover that their adult children may have abandoned the church in which they were raised.

Death is another occasion for people to experience being troubled. Death can cause mental, emotional, spiritual, and physical agitation. We may be disturbed by the suddenness of the death of a family member or a friend. We worry about the deceased's spiritual state. Our physical energy is depleted by our mental and spiritual preoccupation with what we perceive to be our troubles.

Faith in God and in God's Son, Jesus, enables us to let go of our troubles. Whatever causes our distress can be placed in the hands of God if we truly believe that God has everything under control and cares about all of creation. However, if we think that all depends upon us, our plans, then we have made a god of ourselves and fail to profess faith in the God who raised Jesus from the dead.

The troubles which we perceive to exist can throw us off course and make us question the road we have taken. While such questioning is not evil in itself, it can add more weight to our already heavy load of worry. By believing in God and in Jesus we move forward in the face of death, experiencing the comfort and surety of God's words of love, mercy, and care.

Questions for Reflection: What troubles you now? How can God take care of your troubles?

Prayer: God of all, you have instructed me to let go of my troubles and to trust you with all my heart. Give me the faith of Jesus Christ, who trusted you through his death to the new life you gave him. I ask this in his name. Amen.

Journal: What troubles you about death? How is death an opportunity for you to let go and to profess your faith in God and in Jesus?

PSALM A: PS 130

See Part III: Texts of Sacred Scripture—13. Funerals for Adults, Responsorial Psalms, 9. Voice of Christ.

PSALM B: PSS 115 AND 116

See Part III: Texts of Sacred Scripture—13. Funerals for Adults, Responsorial Psalms, 7. Faith, Revelation, Redemption.

Transfer of the Body to the Church or to the Place of Committal

Order of Christian Funerals: par. 120.

SCRIPTURE VERSE A: HIDDEN LIFE

Scripture: (Col 3:3-4) . . . [Y]ou have died, and your life is hidden with Christ in God. When Christ who is your life is revealed, then you also will be revealed with him in glory (3:3-4).

Order of Christian Funerals: par. 120.

Reflection: When I was growing up, my brothers and sisters and cousins and I would play a game called "Hide and Go Seek." After determining who would be "It" first, we would all run off and hide as It covered his or her eyes near some pre-designated "free area" and counted slowly from one to twenty-five. Once the counting was finished, It ventured away from the free area in an attempt to see where we were hidden.

If It got a glimpse of someone's shirt or dress or feet sticking out from behind a tree or bush or car, It would run back to the free area and yell, "One, two, three on (name of person hiding) behind that cedar tree." The goal of the game was to locate each hidden person before he or she was able to come out of hiding, run to the free area, and declare, "One, two, three I'm free!" The first person caught by It became It for the next round of the game.

The last person to be discovered or the final one who had not yet come into the free area was called in by It, saying, "Come out, come out, wherever you are; you're free!" The last person got a thrill knowing that he or she had stayed concealed throughout the whole round of the game and that his or her hiding place had never been discovered.

All our lives we try to see what is hidden. That for which we look is not always visible; sometimes it is mental or spiritual. "Why do I have to work so hard?" is a question seeking a hidden answer. Other questions are like that one: Why do I suffer? Why do I love others? Why do I believe? Why do I not have faith? Why do people die? What does it mean to be alive? Through these and similar questions, we seek for the hidden to be revealed. We want the hidden to come out so that we can know what it is all about.

Life after death is hidden. Death is but a passageway to a hidden life with Christ in God. Whatever makes each of us uniquely who we are passes through death to a hidden life. Faith assures us that what we cannot see indeed exists. God, who lives a hidden life, invites us through death to a similar hidden life.

Some day, when Christ appears in glory, the hidden will be revealed. Some day we will see God as God is. That will be the day that the game of "Hide and Go Seek" will be over. All that has been hidden will be revealed to us.

We stand in the presence of a loved one who has died and gaze upon death, knowing that what we see is not the total picture. We believe that the deceased has crossed over into a hidden life. Death causes separation. Family and friends experiencing this separation can discover themselves viewing death as the end of life, rather than glimpsing the life hidden with Christ in God.

One day, God will say to each of us, "Come out, come out, wherever you are; you're free!" Life on the other side of the grave will no longer be hidden. We will be able to see, and we will be free.

Questions for Reflection: In what ways in this life do you get a glimpse of the life that is hidden on the other side of the grave? What fears do you have about the hidden life after death?

Prayer: Hidden God, you are not visible to my eyes in this life, but you invite me to profess my faith in the resurrection of your Son, Jesus Christ. From the darkness of death you raised him to the light of new life. Strengthen my belief in the hidden life on the other side of the grave as I wait to see you face-to-face. I ask this through Christ the Lord. Amen.

Journal: What do you think the hidden life on the other side of death will be like? What helps you profess your faith in the resurrection?

SCRIPTURE VERSE B: DEATH'S END

Scripture: (Rom 6:8-9) . . . [I]f we have died with Christ, we believe that we will also live with him. We know that Christ, being raised from the dead, will never die again; death no longer has dominion over him (6:8-9).

Order of Christian Funerals: par. 52.

Reflection: There is only one final death, but there are many that lead up to it. Those who have lived can narrate all the deaths they have experienced throughout life. As children, we died when we realized that we could not have every toy in the world. As a teenager, death came when one's first love determined it was time to quit going steady and date other people. Some of the agenda of life written during our twenties died when we approached our mid-forties and realized that no human being could ever do all of "that" in one lifetime. The golden years bring about more deaths through illness or disease, the death of members of our family and friends, and countless other ways.

All of these deaths prepare us for the final one, the big finale for which we have waited all our lives. If we have learned how to die gracefully throughout our lives, then final death will be a celebration. Why? Because it will be indeed the final death. Once we pass through final death, like Christ, we will never die again. Death will have no hold on us.

We live in a death-denying culture. Constantly, others attempt to save us from a little death. If our parents can't buy us all the toys we want, grandparents try. If we fail to make the grade in school because we didn't study enough and get cut from the team, our parents try to bail us out by blaming the coach or promising that we will study harder. Some people experience burnout and nervous breakdowns because they can't give up some of their dreams in order to enjoy a few of them. Final death is pushed off constantly into the far distant future by medical technology. If we fail to learn how to die during our lives, we will be in anguish when we face the inevitable fact of final death some day!

Faith throughout our lives enables us to accept the mystery of life and death and life. We live, we die, and we live again. Following each little death, there is life. And if that wasn't enough, we have the example of Jesus. After he died, God raised him from the dead. He will never die again. Like Jesus, once we experience final death, we will never die again. Death, ironically, is our passageway to life.

Questions for Reflection: What are some little deaths and resurrections that you have experienced? How do those help you face your final death?

Prayer: God of life, when your Son hung his head in death on the cross, you raised him to new life. Now he will never die again. Strengthen my faith in the fullness of life that awaits me. As I experience little deaths and resurrections, give me the grace to prepare for my final death which will set me free from all death so that I may live eternally with you, the Lord Jesus Christ, and the Holy Spirit. Amen.

Journal: In what ways have you been led away from little deaths or ways you have tried to escape little deaths? Was the outcome worse or better than if you had accepted the death, proceeded through it, and gone on with new life? What lessons have you learned from such experiences?

Funeral Liturgy

Order of Christian Funerals: par. 128.

3. Funeral Mass

Order of Christian Funerals: par. 128.

A reflection on each of the readings is found in Part III: Texts of Sacred Scripture—13. Funerals for Adults.

4. Funeral Liturgy Outside Mass

Order of Christian Funerals: par. 177.

A reflection on each of the readings is found in Part III: Texts of Sacred Scripture—13. Funerals for Adults.

Rite of Committal

Order of Christian Funerals: par. 204.

5. Rite of Committal

Order of Christian Funerals: par. 206.

SCRIPTURE VERSE A: COME

Scripture: (Matt 25:34) [Jesus said,] ". . . [T]he king will say to those at his right hand, 'Come, you that are blessed by my Father, inherit the kingdom prepared for you from the foundation of the world . . .'" (25:34).

Order of Christian Funerals: par. 239.

Reflection: "Come" is an invitation. Usually, it is used in phrases like "Come in" or "Come back" or "Come again." As direct address, "you" is implied as the subject of the verb "come." Thus, what we are saying is, "You come in" or "You come back" or "You come again." The invitation makes us feel welcomed, wanted, appreciated.

The narrative of the judgment of the nations in Matthew's Gospel portrays Jesus as the king who has returned in glory and begins the process of judging or separating the sheep from the goats. The goats are sent away, while the sheep are invited to accept the inheritance God has prepared for them from the beginning of creation. They are told "Come," that is, "You come into heaven."

Members of the Christian community can respond to the invitation to "come" by attending the funeral rites for the dead. Their presence surrounding the members of the family and friends of the deceased shows the compassion of Jesus, who felt the pain of the death of his friend Lazarus. In fact, Jesus experienced the agony of death in order to strip it of its power over us. By coming to and participating in the funeral rites, the members of the Christian community function as a sign revealing the love and support of Christ for those who mourn.

The one who has died has accepted the invitation to enter into the kingdom. By gathering around the body, the members of the community declare that they too await the final invitation to come into Christ's kingdom. It is their destiny, prepared for them by God from the beginning of time.

Questions for Reflection: In what ways have you answered the Lord's invitation to "Come"? In what ways do you think you may have failed to respond to it?

Prayer: Compassionate God, through your Son, you have revealed the life you prepared for me from the foundation of the world. Strengthen me with the gift of your Spirit so that I may respond to your invitation and be declared blessed by you. I ask this through Jesus Christ the Lord. Amen.

Journal: In what ways have you been a sign to others of faithful waiting for the final invitation to come into God's reign? In what ways does your lifestyle reflect your destiny?

SCRIPTURE VERSE B: NOTHING LOST

Scripture: (John 6:39) [Jesus said,] ". . . [T]his is the will of him who sent me, that I should lose nothing of all that he has given me, but raise it up on the last day" (6:39).

Order of Christian Funerals: par. 239.

Reflection: Think of all the things we can lose. Coins fall out of our hands and roll under a piece of furniture. They are lost until the next time we move the furniture around. Important papers get filed into the wrong folder and are lost for ever. Women lose pieces of jewelry. Men lose one sock. Children lose pencils. When you think about it, we spend a lot of time losing things.

Jesus assures us that we are not lost. The Johannine Jesus makes it clear that his mission is to keep us from being lost. In fact, it is God's will that no one and no thing should be lost. No human being can be lost and nothing in creation can be lost.

Jesus' promise is that all will be raised up on the last day. The destiny we share with every one and every thing is eternal life. We are always in a state of "being found" says the Johannine Jesus.

Gathering around the body of the person we loved at the place of committal makes us aware of how easy it is to think that death is the end. Once the prayers are finished and the living depart, the body is lowered into the earth or cremated. As the months turn into years and immediate members of the family and friends of the deceased die, it is easy for the dead to be lost. Old tombstones in cemeteries mark the spot of another lost person.

However, Jesus makes it clear that no matter how lost we might be in human eyes, we are never lost from his sight. He assures us that his mission from God was not to lose, but to find. He came to assure us that the dead will be raised to life. In that state beyond the grave, there are no tears and no more loss.

Questions for Reflection: In what ways have you thought about being lost? How has God found you through Christ? What sense of assurance do you get from Jesus' words about being raised up?

Prayer: God of all creation, your will is that nothing you have made should ever be lost. To make that clear, you sent Jesus, your Son, to find me. Through his own death and resurrection, he has revealed the life that awaits me. When I feel lost, fill me with the assurance that I am always found through Jesus Christ the Lord. Amen.

Journal: What have you recently lost and found? How can the action of losing it and finding it help you understand the mission of Jesus to find the lost?

SCRIPTURE VERSE C: CITIZENSHIP

Scripture: (Phil 3:20) . . . [O]ur citizenship is in heaven, and it is from there that we are expecting a Savior, the Lord Jesus Christ (3:20).

Order of Christian Funerals: par. 240.

Reflection: Every person is a citizen on a variety of levels. We are citizens of a country, and, as such, we owe allegiance to a government and receive protection from it. We are citizens of a state or province, and, as such, we support its administrators and receive services from it. Also, we are citizens of a city, town, village, or community, and, as such, we pledge support to the local jurisdiction while exercising our rights and privileges as free people. No matter at what level we view our citizenship, we belong somewhere.

In the United States, we demonstrate our approval of citizenship by pledging allegiance to the flag and standing during the playing of the national anthem. On the state level, we pay our taxes and vote. On the city, town, village, or community level, we get involved in the issues, voicing our opinions and volunteering our time to make where we live a better place for all.

On each level we use our gifts for the good of the whole citizenry. We serve in the armed forces of our country or hold public office. In the state or province in which we live, we may serve as consultors or experts in our respective fields of interest. On the local level, our gifts can be put to work on committees, neighborhood associations, and hundreds of various organizations that rely upon volunteers.

According to Paul's letter to the Philippians, we are citizens of heaven, and as such, we have responsibilities and privileges. One of our responsibilities is to use our gifts in the ministry of consolation to those who grieve the death of a relative or friend. If we are good at cooking, then preparing a meal for the family of the deceased can be the way we share in the ministry of consolation. If we are good at organizing people, then we might volunteer to greet and seat them at the various stations of the funeral liturgy. Those who sing well should lead the music during the vigil service and funeral liturgy. Others can serve, pray, or offer words of consolation according to their individual gifts. By so doing, we exercise our heavenly citizenship and our unity as believers.

We are privileged to share in the citizenship of heaven. God has united us to God's self through the death and resurrection of Jesus Christ. The new covenant, sealed in his blood, has made us citizens of heaven, from where we await his return in glory. The Almighty promises all citizens of heaven that what God did for Jesus—raise him from the dead—the Holy One will do for them. By employing our gifts in the ministry of consolation, we exercise our citizenship now and serve as signs of the new life that awaits us in heaven.

Questions for Reflection: How have you recently served in the ministry of consolation? What gift(s) did you use? How did the use of your gift(s) foster the unity of the members of the community?

Prayer: Compassionate God, through the death and resurrection of Jesus, your Son, you have made me a citizen of heaven. Help me to be a good citizen by using my gifts in the ministry of consolation. Give me a yearning for the coming in glory of the Savior, Jesus Christ, who lives and reigns with you and the Holy Spirit, one God, for ever and ever. Amen.

Journal: What does being a citizen of heaven mean to you? What are your duties or responsibilities as a citizen of heaven? What are the privileges you receive as a citizen of heaven?

SCRIPTURE VERSE D: FIRSTBORN

Scripture: (Rev 1:5-6) . . . Jesus Christ [is] the faithful witness, the firstborn of the dead, and the ruler of the kings of the earth. . . . [T]o him be glory and dominion forever and ever. Amen (1:5a, 6b).

Order of Christian Funerals: par. 266.

Reflection: Usually, the description "firstborn" is applied to the first child to emerge from his or her mother's womb. In the ancient world, the firstborn son was heir to his father's occupation in the community and his family's estate. Today, we describe the firstborn child as the older or eldest of the children born to a woman. No longer is the firstborn the sole heir to occupation or estate. Now, resources are shared among the members of a family.

The author of the Book of Revelation gives the ancient descriptive "firstborn" new meaning when he applies it to Jesus Christ. The unknown apocalyptic writer says that Jesus Christ is "the firstborn of the dead." He is the first to have died and been raised to new life. As a "faithful witness," one who went to his death willingly, he has been exalted as the ruler of the kings of the earth. He is the king of kings because he is the firstborn of the dead. Like the firstborn who emerges from the womb of his or her mother, Jesus is the firstborn from the tomb of mother earth.

When celebrating the rite of committal for adults and children, we are reminded that "the firstborn of the dead" has given us a vision of what awaits all his brothers and sisters who die. God has triumphed over death through the death and resurrection of Jesus Christ and willingly shares that victory with us.

We believe that we became like the "firstborn of the dead" on the day we were baptized. After being plunged into the death-dealing waters, we died, but we were raised up to new life. Our final death completes the process begun with baptism. Through death we pass over to eternal life with Christ, "the firstborn of the dead." As our body is buried or cremated, we become a sign of hope to the living: God will raise us from the dust and ashes to life.

In remembrance of our double deaths, our bodies are sprinkled with water. In the case of a child who was not baptized before he or she died, we do not sprinkle the body with water, but we also do not deny that he or she has passed through death to new life with God. God takes care of all people as God sees fit. We recognize that fact for both the baptized and the non-baptized.

Funerals for the deceased who were not baptized are not meant to diminish the importance of baptism into the Christian community in which faith is nourished. In the case of a child, however, who died before baptism was possible, we do not fail to praise God for God's work in the short life of the child.

Questions for Reflection: How do you share the resources of the community of believers? What hope does Jesus' designation as "firstborn of the dead" give you? What is your vision of being born into eternal life?

Prayer: God of the firstborn of the dead, through your Son's death and resurrection, you have given me an example of faithfulness. Give me the hope of being born again through death to new life with you. Give me a share in Christ's life when I come to the end of my journey on earth. To you, Father, Son, and Holy Spirit, be all glory and dominion for ever and ever. Amen.

Journal: With the understanding that baptism was your first death and that you await your final death, what types of death have you experienced throughout your lifetime? In other words, make a list of your experiences of dying during your process of living.

6. Rite of Committal with Final Commendation

Order of Christian Funerals: par. 205.

The Scripture Verses in the Rite of Committal with Final Commendation are the same as those found in the Rite of Committal above.

PART III

Texts of Sacred Scripture

Part III, "Texts of Sacred Scripture," contains the Scriptural readings and psalms for the celebration of the funeral.

—*Order of Christian Funerals,* par. 343.

13. Funerals for Adults

Old Testament Readings

1. WITNESSING FAITH

Scripture: (Job 19:1, 23-27) [Job said,]

"O that my words were written down!
   O that they were inscribed in a book!
O that with an iron pen and with lead
   they were engraved on a rock forever!
For I know that my Redeemer lives,
   and that at the last he will stand upon the earth;
and after my skin has been thus destroyed,
   then in my flesh I shall see God . . ." (19:23-26).

Order of Christian Funerals: par. 137.

Reflection: How do we proclaim faith in the resurrection? How do we state that we believe that death is not the end of life but a mere passageway to life in a different dimension?

Sometimes people try to prove what they believe about life after death, failing to recognize that faith, by nature of its own definition, has no proof. Books and movies about people who have had near-death experiences abound and are used to "prove" that there is life on the other side of the grave. However, after careful study, it becomes readily apparent that if people have had near-death experiences, they have not died. Near-death means just that—near the gates of death. But the gates didn't open, and for whatever reason, death did not take place and the persons lived.

There is no proof of life after death. We believe there is life after death, and we live according to that faith. Job wanted to profess his faith by having his words written down in a book or chiseled into a permanent stone. By recording his faith in God, whom Job believed would save him from all his misery, the patient man told the whole world about the One whom he trusted.

The death of a member of our community of faith or a member of our family provides the opportunity for us to profess our faith. We gather around the deceased; our presence says that death is not the end. We remember the deeds of the loved one; our memories declare what God has done and continues to do through the life and death of the person. We offer consolation to the members of the family; we proclaim that one day we will be reunited in heaven. Our presence, our remembering, our faith—such witnessing is like words chiseled into a granite stone; it lasts for a long time. It puts into flesh the faith and the hope we proclaim.

Questions for Reflection: What are some of the ways that you have sought proof that there is life after death? How do you profess your faith in life after death?

Prayer: My redeemer, you live in a world beyond my time and space and sight. I profess my faith in you, like words written in a book or chiseled into a stone. Strengthen my weakness and guide me throughout my life, through death, and into life with you. My God, I desire to see your face. Hear this prayer through Jesus Christ, your Son, the Lord. Amen.

Journal: How do you remember the dead of your family and community of faith? How do you console those who are grieving the death of a loved one? How do you witness your faith?

2. RIGHTEOUS (OPTION 1)

Scripture: (Wis 3:1-9 or 3:1-6, 9)

> . . . [T]he souls of the righteous are in the hand of God,
> and no torment will ever touch them.
> In the eyes of the foolish they seemed to have died,
>
> . . . .
>
> but they are at peace (3:1-3).

Order of Christian Funerals: par. 137.

Reflection: Oftentimes, the word "righteous" is confused with "self-righteous," meaning that one is convinced of his or her own correctness in contrast with the actions and beliefs of others. However, in the Bible "righteous" is used to describe a person who acts according to God's law. A "righteous person" is one who is free of sin and guilt. In other words, it is God who declares a person "righteous."

After death, the soul or spirit or personality—whatever it is that makes us who we are—is declared righteous by God. Metaphorically speaking, we are held in the hand of God and all the limitations we experienced in life are removed. Peace is God's gift to us on the other side of death.

The necessities of life seem to bog us down. We must take time to eat and to sleep. We have to work in order to make a living. We get sick, have to see the doctor, get a prescription filled, and go to bed for a few days to recover. We suffer from diseases, such as cancer, AIDS, and hundreds of other afflictions. There are times when people are so bogged down with their limitations that they feel like they are sinking and have no life jacket which will keep their head above the waves.

The hope of being freed from all human limitations on the other side of the grave is what sustains us. Being held in the hand of God, like children on their mothers' laps, comforts us. Being declared righteous by God frees us from the worry about torment, suffering, and death. God offers us the peace which comes from faith that God has everything under control.

Questions for Reflection: In what ways do you feel bogged down by human limitations? How does your faith in life after death help you to live fully even when you may feel like you will be overcome by your limitations?

Prayer: Righteous God, you promise, as you hold me in the palm of your hand, to remove all torment from me in the life to come. When I feel bogged down, lift me up. When I feel overcome, show me the way to your peace. Hear my prayer through Christ the Lord. Amen.

Journal: How has God already declared you to be righteous? Explore the difference between God's naming people righteous and people naming themselves self-righteous.

2.ACCEPTED (OPTION 2)

Scripture: (Wis 3:1-9 or 3:1-6, 9)

> [The] going from us [of the souls of the righteous was thought]
>   to be their destruction
>
> . . . .
>
> [but] God tested them and found them worthy of himself;
> like gold in the furnace he tried them,
> and like a sacrificial burnt offering he accepted them (3:3a,
>   5b-6).

Order of Christian Funerals: par. 143.

Reflection: In the Hebrew Bible (Old Testament), God is often presented in the form of fire, such as the non-consumed burning bush seen by Moses on Mount Horeb. If a person wanted to make an offering to God, it was burned to signify that it belonged wholly to God and was accepted by God. As the flames of the fire licked the offering and gradually turned it to ashes, the God of fire received it.

Today, it is appropriate to say that the fire of youth puts us in contact with God. Young men and women are full of questions, ideals, life, enthusiasm. When a young person dies, we need the consolation offered in the Book of Wisdom. God accepts those who die young. God accepts the fire of youth. The early death of one of the members of a family is a sacrifice acceptable to God. The fire of youth is not extinguished by death.

Automobile accidents, drive-by shootings, gang-related violence, and AIDS claim the lives of many young men and women every year. This life is destroyed, but the next life cannot be wiped out. When God accepts people, God gives them eternal life.

We remember that Jesus was only about thirty years old, at the peak of his maturity, when he suffered a violent death. God accepted him and found him worthy of eternal life. During the funeral for a young man or woman, we remember that God accepts all of us. The Eucharist is our offering of the sacrifice of Christ. As the body of Christ, we entrust ourselves and the person who has died into the hands of God, who accepts all of us, like a burnt offering, and gives us a taste of eternal life.

Questions for Reflection: What young man or woman have you known who has died? How did the fire of his or her youth reflect God to you?

Prayer: God of all gifts, you give me the joy of youth and promise me eternal life. When I am faced with the death of a young man or woman, give me hope that he or she is worthy of you and has been accepted by you, as you accepted the offering of your Son. Grant me a place in heaven, where you live and reign with Jesus Christ and the Holy Spirit, for ever and ever. Amen.

Journal: Recall the death of a young man or woman in your family. How old was he or she? What were the questions, the ideals, and the enthusiasm of his or her life? How do you think those were acceptable to God?

3. GRAY HAIR

Scripture: (Wis 4:7-15)

> . . . [T]he righteous, though they die early, will be at rest.
> For old age is not honored for length of time,
> or measured by number of years;
> but understanding is gray hair for anyone,
> and a blameless life is ripe old age (4:7-9).

Order of Christian Funerals: par. 16.

Reflection: Most societies associate gray hair with age, since the hair on our heads, and for men the hair of their beards and mustaches and on their chests as well, gets grayer and grayer and finally turns white as they grow older. That fact of life makes it easy to figure out the elders in a group of people. We look for those with gray hair. We trust their advice because they have lived more years and accumulated more experience than we have. We look to them for guidance since they have already walked the roads which we see before us.

However, the author of the Book of Wisdom challenges our presupposition that the older someone is the wiser that person is. Age is not necessary for wisdom, just like having gray hair is not necessary for understanding. This perspective on wisdom was formulated long before hair dyes and coloring agents were invented to cover up our gray hair.

Any person who understands is gray. Anyone who is willing to listen to another person's story, entering into the other's life and truly comprehending what he or she says, comes to understand the other. Authentic understanding implies absolute respect for the other person's perspective, even if we strongly disagree with it. Such understanding leads people to say that they will defend the other's right to disagree with them. Understanding is not only gray hair at any age, it is that point of the deepest respect that two people can have for one another.

Blamelessness, says Wisdom, "is a ripe old age." The author doesn't mean that we have to accumulate years before we are blameless, but that we can be without guilt in terms of understanding rather than condemning another. Instead of getting to the heart of another human being, it is easier simply to declare the other wrong and go our merry way. When we engage in condemnation, we indicate that we are still children and without gray hair.

When we are confronted with the death of a young person, especially a teenager, we do well to remember Wisdom's wise words about those who die early and without gray hair. Even though the youth never grayed, he or she may have attained understanding and blamelessness, which in God's eyes are seen to be the same as gray hair and ripe old age.

Questions for Reflection: As you reflect on your relationships with others, do you discover that you understand them or condemn them? In other words, no matter how old you are, do you have any gray hair?

Prayer: Eternal God, you do not measure me by the number of years I have lived nor by the gray I wear on my head. To you, understanding is gray hair and blamelessness is ripe old age. Give me your gift of wisdom so that I might understand and respect others. Make me blamelessly old in your sight. I ask you this through Jesus Christ the Lord. Amen.

Journal: What experiences have you had in your family or in your community of people dying at a young age? After you have thought about a few people who have died young, for each one of them identify their gray hair, degree of understanding, and ripe old age, blamelessness.

4. SWALLOWING UP DEATH

Scripture: (Isa 25:6a, 7-9)

> On this mountain the LORD of hosts will make for all peoples
>   a feast of rich food, a feast of well-aged wines
>
> . . . .
>
> And he will destroy on this mountain
>   the shroud that is cast over all peoples,
>   the sheet that is spread over all nations;
>   he will swallow up death forever (25:6a, 7).

Order of Christian Funerals: par. 154.

Reflection: "God will provide" is an old cliche, yet it contains much truth worth pondering. The prophet Isaiah had the cliche in mind when he wrote that God would make a feast for his people on "this" mountain, a reference to Zion in Jerusalem, the place where God was thought to live. In the context of the passage, the feast is a contrast to the famine and destruction experienced by Israel before it was conquered by its enemies and deported to Babylon in the fifth century B.C.E. The imagery of a feast of fine food and good wine gives hope to the captives of war.

   Also, the prophet contrasts another image: death. In the midst of war there is famine and death. In fact, death hangs over victims of war like a spider's web suspended in a tree. The death web is like a shroud waiting to wrap up its next victim. However, Isaiah proclaims that during the feast on the mountain, God will eat up death forever. Death will be swallowed alive, just as one eats food. The sheet spread over the body of the deceased will be removed to display that death is ended.

   Death is an occasion for a feast. Death is an occasion to celebrate its end. God welcomes the dead to the mountain where the feast awaits. The shroud has no power. The sheet cannot cover the truth that death is no more. Only a life of feasting exists on God's mountain on the other side of death.

Isaiah's words can come alive every time a community is faced with death. They remind people of God's love for them. God loves us into life beyond the grave. The prophet's words can awaken in our hearts our own desire for God's feast and give us assurance that what looks like the end is really the beginning of a banquet on God's mountain. God has defeated death and restored life.

Questions for Reflection: How do Isaiah's words awaken a desire in you to share in God's feast on the other side of death? How do Isaiah's words remind you of God's love for you?

Prayer: God of Zion, you have prepared a feast for me on the mountain where you have chosen to be present to your people. Remove the shroud that causes me to despair. Take away the sheet that hides me from your presence. Give me the grace of your Spirit to trust that death has been swallowed up for ever by the death and resurrection of Jesus Christ, who is Lord for ever and ever. Amen.

Journal: Spend some time with the image of God destroying death by swallowing it during the feast on the mountain. Keep a record of your reflections and feelings about the image.

5. HAVE HOPE (OPTION 1)

Scripture: (Lam 3:17-26)

> . . . [M]y soul is bereft of peace;
>   I have forgotten what happiness is;
> so I say, "Gone is my glory,
>   and all that I had hoped for from the LORD."
>
> . . . .
> But this I call to mind,
>   and therefore I have hope:
> The steadfast love of the LORD never ceases,
>   his mercies never come to an end;
> they are new every morning
>
> . . . .
> It is good that one should wait quietly
> for the salvation of the LORD (3:17-18, 21-23a, 26).

Order of Christian Funerals: par. 154.

Reflection: During the first moments of dealing with the death of a member of our family or a close friend, we can enter into despair. This is true particularly when there seemed to be a lot of hope for recovery. For example, a close friend had open-heart surgery in April and began the process of recovery. She was well enough by June to make a trip to Canada. At Christmas she was doing better than ever. But in January she had another heart attack and died within a few minutes. It was easy to enter into shock and despair. My soul felt like a swimming pool drained for the winter. I was dry. Happiness was forgotten, as I tried to understand the death of my friend.

In such moments, only God remains. The Lord is steadfast. God's love never ceases. When we think that we are the most unlovable, God loves us more. When we think that we have strayed far away, God finds us and brings us back. The mercies of the Lord never end. Like the dawn renewing the light of the day, every morning God renews our lives with hope.

It is not the dead who need hope; it is the living who are desperately in need of hope. The death of another stops us and makes us face our own mortality. Every single person will die one day. Such a thought is enough to depress anyone! However, for believers, Jesus' presence is an assurance that there is life on the other side of the grave. The community of believers enfleshes hope. As people of hope surround us, they strengthen us when we mourn the death of a member of our family or a loved one.

We, the living, can do no more than believe and wait. We can live our hope by our presence to and for those who grieve. We believe that what God did for Jesus after he was put to death on the cross God will do for us: raise us to new life. We wait for the Lord's salvation in the quiet that surrounds the body of the deceased.

Questions for Reflection: When faced with the death of a member of your family or the death of a close friend, what type of depression did you have? How was hope restored to you?

Prayer: God of peace, in the midst of death you restore hope to my soul. Your steadfast love never ceases, and your mercy never comes to an end. In this moment of quiet fill me with the hope of salvation and help me to share it with those who grieve. I ask this through Jesus Christ the Lord in union with the Holy Spirit. Amen.

Journal: In what ways have you experienced hope during a funeral of a member of your family or a close friend? Who was instrumental in sharing hope with you?

5. GRIEF (OPTION 2)

Scripture: (Lam 3:17-26)

. . . [M]y soul is bereft of peace;
I have forgotten what happiness is;

so I say, "Gone is my glory,
   and all that I had hoped for from the LORD."
The thought of my affliction and my homelessness
   is wormwood and gall!
My soul continually thinks of it
   and is bowed down within me (3:17-20).

Order of Christian Funerals: par. 14.

Reflection: No matter who leads the various rites of prayer associated with the death and committal of a person, he or she is a minister of comfort, offering consolation to the community of believers, especially to the family of the dead person. This ministry of comfort is important no matter what the age of the deceased. However, it is critical for the members of the family of a person who died at an early age, such as a teenager, a young adult, or one in the middle years.

Grief is complex. Its expression varies from person to person and from one occasion of death to another. In grieving the death of a teenager, the mourning of each parent will be unique because each had a different relationship to the son or daughter. If the teen died in an automobile accident, the suddenness of the loss may not impact the parents immediately and their grief will flow later. If the youth died of AIDS, society's attitudes may magnify the grief. Parents and friends of the young person may struggle with the emotions of guilt, fear, shame, and abandonment. In the case of a suicide, the survivors may grieve by blaming themselves for not recognizing the signs given by the person contemplating suicide, or they may be angry with the dead person for having brought about his or her own death. The lack of an answer to the question "Why?" adds to the intensity of feelings.

The sudden heart failure of a young athlete or the heart attack of a spouse brings disorientation for members of the family. In the former case, people grieve by talking about the circumstance of the death, the feelings of loss, the suddenness of no longer having the person around. In the latter case, a person has lost a part of himself or herself. He or she feels alone and lonely, recalls the special things missed about the spouse, and experiences surges of tears at unexpected times, but especially on special days, such as birthdays, anniversaries, and holidays.

Grief gnaws on people emotionally; they speak about being upset or angry. It attacks them physically; they are not hungry, may lose weight, may feel cold. Spiritually, grief causes us to ask, "Why, God?" When mourning, people are psychologically not balanced, sometimes they are not able to accept the death as real. Mentally, grief impairs clear thinking.

Grieving, the open expression of thoughts and emotions regarding the death of a loved one, is a journey that takes lots of work. It requires energy and effort for healing. One person's experience can be compared to another's only in the most general of ways since grief is unique to each individual. The members of the community of believers walk with those who grieve after death, during the funeral rites, and for years afterward. The support offered to the mourners begins with the words and actions of the ministers of comfort, which implies listening, being with, supporting, and not having all the answers. Sometimes, the best comfort is silence.

Questions for Reflection: Think about two members of your family who have died. How did you grieve for each of them? How was your grieving different for each? In what ways are you still grieving?

Prayer: God of comfort, in the disorientation of my mourning you offer me the peace that the hope of eternal life brings. When I am bowed down, lift me up. When I feel lost and alone, help me to know your presence. Fill the void of my emptiness with the joy of the Holy Spirit, who lives and reigns with you and Jesus Christ, for ever and ever. Amen.

Journal: In what ways have you, as a member of the Christian community, supported the grieving family of someone who has died? In what ways have you, as a member of the Christian community, experienced the support of other members of the church while you were mourning the death of a member of your family?

6. DUST AWAKENS

Scripture: (Dan 12:1-3) . . . [A]t that time your people shall be delivered, everyone who is found written in the book. Many of those who sleep in the dust of the earth shall awake, some to everlasting life, and some to shame and everlasting contempt. Those who are wise shall shine like the brightness of the sky, and those who lead many to righteousness, like the stars forever and ever (12:1c-3).

Order of Christian Funerals: par. 6.

Reflection: I have spent a lot of time thinking about dust. I have thought about dust not because it settles on my tables and bookshelves or on the tile on my front porch. Dust has been in my thoughts because of all the funerals I have celebrated for members of my family and friends. I have been thinking about human dust.

In the past ten years, I have buried my father, my mother, my "second mother," maternal grandfather and grandmother, an uncle, my first great-niece, and a nun-friend. At each of their graves, on behalf of the community, I prayed: ". . . [W]e commend to Almighty God our brother/sister . . . and we commit his/her body to the ground . . . earth to earth, ashes to ashes, dust to dust" (*Order of Christian Funerals*, par. 219). I became aware that all of them are in the process of returning to that out of which they were made: dust.

Every year on Ash Wednesday, we, literally, come face to face with dust—ashes. We are told to remember that we are dust and to dust we will return. Dust reminds us that all things are not permanent. Dust reminds us that we are not permanent.

We might look like we are sleeping as we are waked in our casket, but that painted smile on our faces and the hands holding the rosary will all too quickly become a pile of calcium and ultimately nothing. A few years in the grave and there will be little if any trace of us left—just earth to earth, ashes to ashes, dust to dust.

It is good for us to come into direct contact with our dustiness. We need to remember who we really are, to reflect on what we are—or aren't. We are not permanent fixtures here, although we often live like we will be here forever, and we pretend that death will never touch us. But the truth of the matter is we are only passing through. One day during those last moments of life, those last seconds before we go back into dust, we will have the opportunity to entrust ourselves into the hands of the invisible God, the only one who can awaken dust.

Realizing that we are dust enables us to let go of everything we think is important and embrace the God who guarantees that we will be like stars in the sky. Letting go, we can let God help us face the fact of our mortality and our dusty future. We are one when it comes to dust.

Questions for Reflection: What is positive about dust? How do you think the common future of all people—dust—bonds us together spiritually?

Prayer: God of everlasting life, you promise that one day those who sleep in the dust of the earth will awaken. Strengthen that common bond among all your people. Give me hope that as I sleep in dust you will one day awaken me to share your life in the new heavens and the new earth where death will be no more. Hear this prayer through Jesus Christ the Lord. Amen.

Journal: Which members of your family or friends have died in the past few years? In what ways are they still united to you? How did their lives and deaths enrich your life?

7. PRAYING FOR THE DEAD

Scripture: (2 Macc 12:43-46) [Judas Maccabeus] took up a collection . . . and sent it to Jerusalem to provide for a sin offering. In doing this he acted very well and honorably, taking account of the resurrection. For if he were not expecting that those who had fallen would rise again, it would have been superfluous and foolish to pray for the dead (12:43-44).

Order of Christian Funerals: par. 6.

Reflection: We pray both for and with the dead. We pray to God for the dead, asking for mercy and requesting forgiveness of the deceased's sins. Knowing that no human being is perfect, we implore God's clemency in the light of human limitations and the inability to rise to a state of perfection. Like a teacher takes an eraser and makes the words on the board vanish, God speaks forgiveness and removes the guilt of the dead.

The dead pray for us. Because the bonds of communion cannot be broken by death, the deceased can intercede for us with God. They can pray on our behalf, seeking God's mercy and forgiveness of sins for us. Because they have lived in our time and space, our loved ones who have died understand our limitations and inability to be perfect, and they plead for us with God.

The communion of saints is the name we give to the union that exists between the Church on earth and the Church in heaven. As we look for the resurrection of the dead, in every Mass we pray in union with the whole Church, with Mary, the apostles, the martyrs, the saints. We remember those who have died; they went before us marked with the sign of faith and with the hope of rising again. Referred to as those who sleep in Christ, we ask God to give them light, happiness, and peace. Almost in the same breath we ask God to give us fellowship with them, even though we are sinners. All we can do is trust in God's mercy and love as the saints intercede on our behalf. Only God knows the faith of the dead, just as only God knows the faith of the living.

Just as the dead sleep in Christ and go to their rest trusting that God will raise them from the dead, we await the day of our death and our final sleep in Christ, trusting that what God did for Jesus God will do for us.

Questions for Reflection: For which deceased members of your family or friends do you pray? How do they pray for you?

Prayer: Merciful God, when my human limitations bog me down, raise me up in your forgiving arms of love. Strengthen my faith in the resurrection of your Son, Jesus Christ. Keep me in union with your Church on earth and in heaven. I ask this through Jesus Christ the Lord. Amen.

Journal: Besides praying for and with the dead, what other actions demonstrate your communion with those who have fallen asleep in Christ? How do the deceased show their union with you?

New Testament Readings

1. NO PARTIALITY (OPTION 1)

Scripture: (Acts 10:34-43 or 10:34-36, 42-43) [Peter said to Cornelius and his household,] "I truly understand that God shows no partiality, but in every nation anyone who fears him and does what is right is acceptable to him" (10:34-35).

Order of Christian Funerals: par. 18.

Reflection: God is not biased, but, sometimes, people are. God accepts all people who do what is right, meaning that they love and respect every human person as an image of God. From God's point of view, there is no room for partiality.

Often, however, people are partial. Bias shows up in terms of skin color. A white man gets a job for which a black man is more qualified; someone showed partiality. A man receives a promotion in a company and a more qualified woman is ignored; bias triumphs. Those who are gay or lesbian are treated as inferior to those who are heterosexual; prejudice wins.

There is also a type of partiality which I call religious haughtiness. Those who practice one religion have a tendency to think that they possess absolute truth and condemn all other religions as inferior to their own. Even within religions different denominations practice a haughtiness which sets the members of one church in a position superior to the members of another church. Religious adherents demonstrate partiality.

The great lesson that Peter learned is that God is not partial to any skin color, sex, or religion. God accepts all people who know

God and love one another with the same respect for human dignity that God shows.

The church demonstrates the equal human dignity of all human beings in permitting the use of the funeral rites for a baptized member of another church. Certainly, if the deceased had expressed wishes contrary to what the members of his or her family propose, the use of the *Order of Christian Funerals* would not be appropriate. But when the minister of another church is not available, such as in mission territory or when a congregation is seeking a new pastor, the church, at the discretion of the local bishop, permits the use of its rites for the deceased.

Both in life and in death God shows no partiality. Those who profess their faith in a God who is not biased must live according to God's ways. God understands people; people must understand people.

Questions for Reflection: What are some of your personal biases? How do those affect your relationship with others? How do they inhibit you from showing basic human respect for others?

Prayer: Impartial God, anyone who loves you and does what is right is acceptable to you. Increase my love for you. Make me aware of my biases so that I can remove them. Give me a deeper respect for the human dignity of all people, both those alive and those who have died. I ask this through Jesus Christ the Lord. Amen.

Journal: In what ways have you and/or your church been found guilty of religious haughtiness? How can you come to a better understanding of other denominations or religions without making them inferior to your own?

1. FAITH (OPTION 2)

Scripture: (Acts 10:34-43 or 10:34-36, 42-43) [Peter said to Cornelius and his household:] ". . . God anointed Jesus of Nazareth with the Holy Spirit and with power; . . . he went about doing good and healing all who were oppressed by the devil, for God was with him. We are witnesses to all that he did both in Judea and in Jerusalem. They put him to death by hanging him on a tree; but God raised him on the third day and allowed him to appear, not to all the people but to us who were chosen by God as witnesses, and who ate and drank with him after he rose from the dead" (10:38-41).

Order of Christian Funerals: par. 12.

Reflection: Faith is radical trust in God. The trust that we place in other people is like the trust that we have in God. Husband and wife build trust in each other through the years of their marriage. The man believes the woman when she says that she will take care of paying the bills one month. The woman trusts the man when he says that he will see to the car's maintenance. However, they also trust each other with their hearts; they do not fear to share their innermost feelings of joy and sorrow, happiness and pain with each other. All of their small acts of trust reach a crescendo in the act of intercourse as they give themselves to each other in love.

However, unlike people, who can be seen, God is invisible. That is why faith is radical trust in God. People live their faith in their own way, usually in relationship to a community of fellow believers. Through life experiences, they grow in trusting God. Faith reaches a crescendo as we die and entrust ourselves into the hands of God and trust that what God did for Jesus God will do for us: raise us from the dead.

In celebrating the funeral liturgy, the focus is the faith of the person who has died. The author of the Acts of the Apostles, the same one who wrote Luke's Gospel, records the early proclamation of faith made by the Christian community: God raised Jesus from the dead. The simplicity of that faith is not meant to diminish the importance of creeds and doctrines, but in the case of a teenager who has died in an accident or from cancer or some other disease, the application of that simple proclamation to the teen's life may be appropriate.

Usually, young men and women do not know a lot about creeds and doctrines and may not consider them all that important, even if they have studied them. The faith of the teenager may have been as simple as the early Church's proclamation that God raised Jesus from the dead. In the person's own way, he or she trusted God. Developing trust in God is a lifetime process of exploration, discernment, and being led by God. Young men and women of faith trust God insofar as they are able.

So at funerals of young people, we celebrate whatever faith they had, not what we wish they had. The simplest faith is sufficient in God's eyes. By inviting the members of the Christian community to reflect on a teen's faith, its members, especially its younger members, may grow in their radical trust in God.

Questions for Reflection: What young man or woman have you known who has died? What type of faith did he or she have? How did that faith help you grow in your radical trust in God?

Prayer: God of Jesus, you anointed your Son with the Holy Spirit and sent him forth to proclaim the good news of your reign. In you he placed his trust, and you raised him from the dead to new life with you. Give me the gift of your Spirit and help me to grow in my trust in you. I make this prayer through Jesus Christ, the risen Lord. Amen.

Journal: Look back through your life's events. What experiences helped you grow in trust in God? How would you characterize your faith before and after each of those experiences?

2. RECONCILED

Scripture: (Rom 5:5-11) . . . God proves his love for us in that while we still were sinners Christ died for us. . . . [I]f while we were enemies, we were reconciled to God through the death of his Son, much more surely, having been reconciled, will we be saved by his life. But more than that, we even boast in God through our Lord Jesus Christ, through whom we have now received reconciliation (5:8, 10-11).

Order of Christian Funerals: par. 13.

Reflection: All of us are sinners. Certainly, there is nothing new in that statement. We experience our sinful selves every day of our lives. Instead of telling the total truth, we tip-toe around it in an effort not to upset someone. We see the homeless walking down the street and think that government is not doing its job to take care of them. The idea that it might be our job to minister to the needs of the homeless may never cross our minds. We misuse our wealth to buy whatever we want, never realizing that the more we have the more isolated we are from the rest of the human community. Yes, all of us are sinners.

And yet all of us are reconciled to God through the death of Jesus. Indeed, that is a new thought. Whatever kept us from God—sin, blindness, stupidity—has been removed, cleared away, by the death of Jesus. In the death of the Son, God saw division erased and union restored. As a mediator, Jesus brought God and people to the bargaining table and offered himself as the price for reconciliation.

Not to be overlooked is the reconciliation accomplished between people and people. Not only did God reconcile us to God, but the Merciful One also removed the differences between us. Whatever kept us from each other—prejudice, bias, stubbornness—has been removed, erased, by the death of Jesus. The human community is one again because of the death of one human being.

There is still more good news. God has saved us by the life of Jesus. When we were about to fall off the cliff of self-centeredness into the canyon of self-destruction below, God built a Jesus-bridge. Now we can cross over that bridge from death to life with the assurance that we will not perish. God has saved us for ever. Death is nothing other than crossing over Jesus to life with God.

Certainly, such reconciliation and salvation were undeserved. We did nothing to merit them. If we could have won them, there would have been no need for God to send the reconciling and saving Jesus to earth. All we can do is boast about what God has done for us.

Frequently, the death of a member of our family or a friend sparks our awareness of God's gifts. God's free gift of grace moves people during the time of death to seek reconciliation with each other and to renew the ties which bind them together as a human family. In other words, the death of a loved one may accomplish in some small degree what the death of Jesus accomplished for the whole world—reconciliation, salvation, and peace.

Questions for Reflection: Whose death sparked reconciliation in your family? How was that reunion of people celebrated?

Prayer: God of grace, when I was still a sinner, you saved me from death and gave me life through the death of your Son, Jesus. The reconciliation he gave to me spreads to others when I am willing to reconcile differences with them. I thank you for such an undeserved gift, and I praise you through Jesus Christ in the unity of the Holy Spirit for ever and ever. Amen.

Journal: Where have you witnessed the reconciliation of God and people and people and people taking place? Why do you think death can be an occasion for reconciliation? How do you praise God for the gift of reconciliation?

3. MYSTERY

Scripture: (Rom 5:17-21) . . . [J]ust as one man's trespass led to condemnation for all, so one man's act of righteousness leads to justification and life for all. For just as by the one man's disobedience the many were made sinners, so by the one man's obedience the many will be made righteous (5:18-19).

Order of Christian Funerals: par. 2.

Reflection: When we hear the word "mystery," we often think that it refers to that which cannot be explained. "It's a great mystery," we say, when we must answer a question about how the television or radio works, how a digital watch displays the time, how a photograph in a computer in Washington, D.C., can be transferred digitally through a telephone line to San Francisco, California. However, from a biblical point of view, mystery refers to God's activity. And from that perspective, we might be able to attempt to answer the "how," but we cannot even begin to answer the "why."

How did we get into the mess that we found ourselves in? The answer to that question, given by Paul in his letter to the Romans, is simple: The first man and woman trespassed through the Garden of Eden and ate of the tree of the knowledge of good and evil. Their disobedience and desire to be like God made all of us disobey and want to be like God. In other words, their story is retold in every human life.

Paul answers the next question, How did we get out of that human mess?, by saying that God created a new person, one who would do what is right because it is the right thing to do. Paul calls this righteousness. Jesus, the Son of God, did not desire to be like God. He obeyed and did not eat of the tree of the knowledge of good and evil, but was nailed to the tree of the cross as a demonstration of his faithfulness to doing God's will.

It is God's work in Jesus Christ that is the mystery. It is God's work in Jesus Christ that cannot be explained. Why did God choose one human being to justify all people? Why did one human being's death and resurrection make righteous all people? The only answer we can begin to give is, because God wanted to grace us in that way.

The mystery of the death and resurrection of Jesus is etched onto the world again every time someone dies. In a much smaller degree, the death of a member of our family or a friend reminds us of the justification and life given to us by God in Christ. The member of our family or friend who shared God's grace with us during life continues to share it through death and new life. One human being's righteous lifestyle continues the process of uniting people and God that God began in Christ. There is no answer to why God does this. God's saving actions are a mystery.

Questions for Reflection: In whose death have you recently recognized the mystery of Jesus Christ's death and resurrection? Explain. How has the life and death of the deceased brought new life to you?

Prayer: Mysterious God, the disobedience of the first man and woman brought me condemnation, but the obedience of Jesus, your Son, brought me justification and life. Help me to know your will and give me the strength and courage to do it. Make my life an example of your righteousness. I ask this through Jesus Christ the Lord. Amen.

Journal: How is your life a reflection of the obedience of Jesus? How does your example of living God's will influence others to be righteous? Identify the mystery of God's work in your life.

4. INITIATED INTO DEATH (OPTION 1)

Scripture: (Rom 6:3-9 or 6:3-4, 8-9) Do you not know that all of us who have been baptized into Christ Jesus were baptized into his death? Therefore we have been buried with him by baptism into death, so that, just as Christ was raised from the dead by the glory of the Father, so we too might walk in newness of life (6:3-4).

Order of Christian Funerals: par. 2.

Reflection: Most people have had some experience of initiation. Through a series of rites, ceremonies, or ordeals we become a member of a group. For example, college fraternities and sororities are famous for the ordeals men and women must endure in order to become a member of the group. Those desiring initiation will bow down in homage to the members of the group, clean their rooms, scrub bathrooms and floors, wear humiliating clothing, and do just about anything to be declared a member of the group. Likewise, persons who want to join civic service organizations, such as the Elks Club, Lions Club, or Rotary Club, may pay an initiation fee to join or take part in a ritual of receiving a badge or pin.

Baptism, confirmation, and Eucharist comprise the sacrament of initiation for Christians. A person is dunked in water, smeared with oil, dressed in new clothes, given a candle, and fed bread and wine. To the outside observer, the initiation ceremonies look rather odd. However, to the insider, the rituals not only make others members of the Christian community, but make present in their life the mystery of the death and resurrection of Jesus.

On the day of baptism, we were plunged simultaneously into death and new life. We went down into the waters of the baptismal pool, were drowned, and raised up. Upon us was traced the death and resurrection of Jesus. The chrism oil poured on our heads further emphasized that we had been "Christed," made a member of the Spirit-filled body of Christ. And if that weren't enough, if we were baptized as adults, we approached the table of the Lord's body and blood, in the words of St. Augustine, to become what we already were: the body of Christ. If we were baptized as infants, we prepared to receive the Eucharist at an age when we better understood what it means to eat and drink at Christ's table. And at some time after that, we were confirmed, renewed in the Spirit poured out on us on the day of our baptism.

However, while we were initiated into the community of faith, we also died for the first time. We had the mystery of the Lord's death traced on us in the sign of the cross. Initiation began a process of dying that would take a lifetime. When we celebrate a funeral, we return to our initiation roots and remember the lifetime of dying and rising that the deceased has completed. The body is sprinkled with water to remind us both of the time death began and the fact it leads ultimately to eternal life. The casket is covered with the white robe of baptism. The Easter candle, from which the dead received the light of Christ at baptism, is placed near the coffin. And the members of the family and friends of our loved one gather around the body and celebrate Eucharist, the action of making present the body of Christ, an action in which the deceased participated countless times.

The funeral is an initiation for the deceased. They are initiated into that life on the other side of death, into that communion of the saints, into that world where Christ, whom God raised from the dead, offers life that is new and never-ending.

Questions for Reflection: How many times have you died and experienced new life since you were initiated into the Christian community? Into what group were you initiated? In whose funeral initiation rites have you participated? Did you experience more death or more life? Explain.

Prayer: God of death and life, you initiated your Son, Jesus, into risen life through his death on the cross. On the day of my baptism, I died and rose with him. Continue to trace in me the mystery of Jesus. Prepare me for the day of my death, when I will die for the last time and be raised to the newness of life you share with the Lord Jesus Christ and the Holy Spirit, for ever and ever. Amen.

Journal: In what ways can you understand death to be a life-giving experience? How do you understand a funeral to be an initiation ritual?

4. INITIATED INTO DEATH (OPTION 2)

Scripture: (Rom 6:3-9 or 6:3-4, 8-9) . . . [I]f we have died with Christ, we believe that we will also live with him. We know that Christ, being raised from the dead, will never die again; death no longer has dominion over him (6:8-9).

Order of Christian Funerals: par. 2.

Reflection: From preschool through high school, youths are involved in all types of initiations, which continue through college and into their adult lives. Children have clubs into which they are initiated by learning the secret code word. In junior high and high school, young men and women are initiated into athletic and academic teams through practice. Fraternities and sororities become the focus for initiation during the college years. After we settle down, we may be initiated into the Knights of Columbus or the Daughters of Isabella, the Kiwanis Club, the Elks Club, or any other service organization.

Every time we are initiated, we leave some of our life behind and begin a new one. Something of us dies, such as time spent at something else, and a new aspect begins, such as participation on a team or living in a fraternity or sorority house. We usually refer to the interaction of dying and living as growth. Leaving behind bits of our childhood and teen years and youth, we are enriched by the new life we discover on our journey.

The sacraments of initiation—baptism, confirmation, and Eucharist—mark moments of religious initiation. Many people are baptized when they are infants. They receive the Eucharist for the first time in either first or second grade, and they are confirmed during their high school years. Once initiation in the church is complete, new experiences of God await.

The choice of some of life's vocations are marked sacramentally. After deciding on a marriage partner, the sacrament of matrimony seals the dying of each partner to his and her old life and celebrates the new life ahead of the couple. Ordination to any one of the three levels of the clergy—deacons, priests, bishops—includes the prostration of the candidate on the floor, as if he were dead, to indicate leaving behind his old life and beginning a new one as a minister in the church. While not a sacrament, religious profession of vows entails dying to one's old life and rising to a new one.

When young men or women die suddenly, such as in an automobile accident, or by some violent act, such as a drive-by shooting or suicide, they experience initiation into eternal life with God. The suddenness of the death causes great grief and mental trauma for family members, friends, school mates, teachers. They need to mourn the loss of the loved one. They have experienced a sudden and unexpected traumatic death with which few people can sympathize.

As the family members, friends, schoolmates, teachers work out their grief, we join them in marking the initiation of the dead into life with God. Through the use of water, the pall, and the Easter Candle, we remember the young person's baptism. Through the funeral liturgy, we remember the deceased's first Eucharist. By recalling those religious initiations, we join the family and friends in proclaiming that the youth has been initiated into eternal life through death.

Questions for Reflection: In what religious initiation have you recently participated? What part of life was left behind? What new life was embraced? How do you die and rise with Christ every time you celebrate the Eucharist?

Prayer: God of Jesus, after your Son's death on the cross, you initiated him into new life by raising him from the dead. Teach me the mystery of his death and life. Trace it in my life. Through my death, initiate me into the eternal life you share with Jesus Christ and the Holy Spirit, one God, for ever and ever. Amen.

Journal: Recall several initiations you have experienced during your life. For each identify what bit of life you left behind and what new life you embraced. How do those experiences help you to trust that death is not the end but the beginning of new life with Christ?

5. LABOR PAINS

Scripture: (Rom 8:14-23) We know that the whole creation has been groaning in labor pains until now; and not only the creation, but we ourselves, who have the first fruits of the Spirit, groan inwardly while we wait for adoption, the redemption of our bodies (8:22-23).

Order of Christian Funerals: par. 35.

Reflection: Labor pains are caused by the contractions of the muscles of a woman's uterus forcing her child through the birth canal and into the world. Labor pains herald the birth of a child.

However, all of us are always in labor pains. While it might not at first sound like a pleasant thought, on the day we were baptized, we began a process of simultaneously being born and giving birth. Through the womb of the Church, the baptismal font, we began a birthing process which will not end until the day we die, are placed in a womb-like coffin, and placed into mother earth's womb. The Easter candle, from which our light came on the day of baptism, is placed near our coffin-womb as others declare that we have been born into new life. In other words, those who loved us declare that we will be re-created.

While we are in the lifetime process of being born, we also give birth. As members of the Church, we give visible and living shape to the Church, the assembly of believers. When we initiate others into the Church, we share our Spirit and groan inwardly as we give birth to them. The initiates stretch us, challenge us, offer their gifts to us, and we share the birth pangs of new life.

The interaction of being born and giving birth places us in the position of waiting for adoption, the fullness of redemption. We already share in Christ's victory over death and his resurrection through our own death in the baptismal pool and resurrection from it. We already share in Christ's victory over death and his resurrection through our giving birth to others, a type of raising them to new life. What the fullness of redemption will look like, we do not know. Now, we grown inwardly, waiting to be re-created, reborn on the other side of death. Until that happens, our loved ones who have died rest secure with the presence of Christ in their womb-tombs.

Questions for Reflection: What labor pains do you experience in being born? What labor pains do you experience in giving birth? What does redemption mean for you?

Prayer: God of all creation, you gave birth to people by forming them from the dust of the earth and breathing the breath of your Spirit into them. Through the waters of baptism, you have re-created me. Enable me to share in the labor of giving birth to others in your Church. Bring all your people to the fullness of redemption through Jesus Christ the Lord. Amen.

Journal: What people have helped you to be born over and over again? What labor pains did you have? What people have you helped to be born? What labor pains did you have? Do you think that death will be your last labor pain? Explain.

6. NOTHING CAN SEPARATE

Scripture: (Rom 8:31b-35, 37-39) If God is for us, who is against us? He who did not withhold his own Son, but gave him up for all of us, will he not with him also give us everything else? . . . I am convinced that neither death, nor life, nor angels, nor rulers, nor things present, nor things to come, nor powers, nor height, nor depth, nor anything else in all creation, will be able to separate us from the love of God in Christ Jesus our Lord (8:31b-32, 38-39).

Order of Christian Funerals: par. 27.

Reflection: We live in a world which thrives on division instead of unity. If you think about it, you will see that we spend most of our time defending our divisions into countries, states, political groups, religions, churches, social groups, and on and on. Separation in the hope of being able to define a person is the practice of the day.

But what happens if we begin to think from the other end of the division-unity pole? Starting with the unity of all people and looking for commonality enables us, not only to live together in peace, but to discover that others enrich our lives. A wonderful sharing of people and resources takes place when we begin with unity instead of division.

When we first look at it, death might seem to be a dividing force. After all, loved ones are dead; they are no longer breathing, no longer have brain waves, no longer have heart beats. But death is not a separation of the dead from the living. Death is a participation in life; it is an aspect of living through which we enter into a new plane of existence while maintaining our unity with all that God has created.

The God who loves all of us into being will not permit us to be separated. God is a God of unity. Such lack of division was demonstrated in the death of Jesus. The crucifixion did not separate him from the earth, as some thought. His death plunged him into more life and the love of God which unites all of us.

The deceased person shared in the unity of God through Christ before death and continues to share in it after death. Nothing can separate us from each other. God's unity is greater than people's division.

Questions for Reflection: How do you, consciously or unconsciously, focus on separation rather than unity? How can you change your point of view so that you begin with the unity of all people?

Prayer: God of all, your love for me is greater than anything that tries to separate me from you. Nothing in the past, nothing in the present, nothing in the future can divide what you have united. When faced with death, strengthen me with the love you share as Trinity: Father, Son, and Holy Spirit, one God, for ever and ever. Amen.

Journal: How has God loved you into unity with others? Make a list of some of your recent experiences of unity. For each experience identify how God's love was manifested to you and how that love pushed you to avoid separation.

7. BELONGING TO CHRIST

Scripture: (Rom 14:7-9, 10b-12) We do not live to ourselves, and we do not die to ourselves. If we live, we live to the Lord, and if we die, we die to the Lord; so then, whether we live or whether we die, we are the Lord's. For to this end Christ died and lived again, so that he might be Lord of both the dead and the living (14:7-9).

Order of Christian Funerals: par. 8.

Reflection: There is no doubt that every person who ever lived, who is alive now, and who will live is unique. As a unique individual, each of us is separated from all other unique individuals. No two of us are exactly alike—even identical twins—and so we are all alone in a sense. Our individual uniqueness tends to isolate us, whether we are conscious of it or not.

Our society fosters and caters to our individuality. We are given the right to life, to freedom, to pursue happiness. Those basic rights and others like them are guaranteed to us by the Constitution of the United States. Because we take our individual rights so seriously, and, indeed, we should, we tend to put ourselves first in our thoughts and our actions. So when we consider whether or not we should buy a new TV, we implicitly ask, "What's in it for me?" When we are confronted with a moral question, our answer may depend upon what's in it for me. Sometimes, the question indicating self-concern is phrased, "How can I win?" or "What do I have to do to get ahead?" No matter how it is asked, the answer will lean heavily toward the good that will accrue to me.

Death puts our individuality into the context of the community. No matter how individually alone each person is, he or she belongs to the whole Church, the whole community, the whole body of Christ. Through the waters of baptism, we were plunged into a community of individuals who look to each others' needs before their individual needs. While we live, we belong to the community, the visible manifestation of Christ, the body of Christ in the world today. When we die, we still belong to the community.

It makes no difference whether an individual is alive or dead, since Christ is Lord of all. Baptism, our first death, focused us on living for the Lord and his body-church. Death focuses us on a continuity of living for the Lord and his community of believers. No matter whether individuals are alive or dead, they belong to someone (Christ) and something (community) that is greater.

We did not lose our individuality in baptism, and we do not lose it in death. We have it refocused. Instead of asking, "What's in it for me?" we ask, "How will this affect the whole body of Christ?" We are responsible for one another. When we serve others, the body of Christ, we serve ourselves as members of that body.

Questions for Reflection: In what ways have you recently put yourself first and the body of Christ second? In what ways have you put the community first and yourself second?

Prayer: God of the living and the dead, no matter whether I live or die, I belong to Christ, your Son. Remove all selfish individuality from me. Guide my life and my death so that I might live and die for him who died and rose and is Lord of both the dead and the living, Jesus Christ, reigning for ever and ever. Amen.

Journal: Recently, what have you done that indicates that you are responsible for the other members of the body of Christ, the Church? How has your uniqueness, your individuality, benefitted others?

8. LIGHT OF CHRIST

Scripture: (1 Cor 15:20-23, 24b-28 or 15:20-23) . . . Christ has been raised from the dead, the first fruits of those who have died. For since death came through a human being, the resurrection of the dead has also come through a human being; for as all die in Adam, so all will be made alive in Christ. But each in his own order: Christ the first fruits, then at his coming those who belong to Christ. . . . The last enemy to be destroyed is death (15:20-23, 26).

Order of Christian Funerals: par. 35.

Reflection: The funeral of a deceased relative or friend presents the opportunity for us to proclaim our faith in the resurrection of Christ. We believe that God raised Jesus from the dead. Just as death came into the world through the first human beings to be created, new life after death has come into the world through the most perfect of human beings, Jesus Christ. When God raised Jesus from the dead, God also raised from the dead all those who believe in him.

We begin celebrating Christ's resurrection during the Easter Vigil on Holy Saturday night. In between the sunset of Holy Saturday and the sunrise of Easter Sunday, we gather in the darkness of the death of night and light a large candle. The Easter candle is a sign of the resurrection of Christ. Its light scatters the darkness of the night and illumines the way for those who follow Christ. Usually lit from a fire made outside the church, the Easter candle leads the worshipers into the building as they sing, "Christ our light." The resurrection of Christ gives light to the night. The resurrection of Christ destroys the enemy called death.

During the vigil service for the deceased, if it is held in the church, and during the funeral liturgy, the Easter candle is placed near the coffin of the deceased. The large burning candle reminds the living that Christ is present. It also proclaims that the person who has died has passed through death to life with the risen Lord. Just as Jesus died and became the first to rise, so another human being has died and been raised to eternal life. Once again, the enemy of death has been destroyed.

What looks like death—a lifeless body in a casket—is transformed into a sign of life by the Easter candle. In the midst of death's darkness, the light of new life shines. We proclaim our faith in the resurrection as we stare death in the face and see life.

Questions for Reflection: In what ways has a deceased relative or friend been a light for you? How has his or her death strengthened your faith in the resurrection?

Prayer: God of light, your only-begotten Son, Jesus Christ, died on the cross, but you raised him from the dead and made him the first fruits of those who have died. Strengthen my faith in his resurrection. Destroy death in me that I may shine with the light of the risen Christ, who lives and reigns with you and the Holy Spirit, one God, for ever and ever. Amen.

Journal: Light a single candle in a dark room and spend some quiet time with it. What feelings does the light bring to you? How does the light help you believe in the death and resurrection of Christ?

9. VICTORY

Scripture: (1 Cor 15:51-57) We will not all die, but we will all be changed. . . . For this perishable body must put on imperishability, and this mortal body must put on immortality. When this perishable body puts on imperishability, and this mortal body puts on immortality, then the saying that is written will be fulfilled:

> "Death has been swallowed up in victory."
> "Where, O death, is your victory?
> Where, O death, is your sting?" (15:51b, 53-55).

Order of Christian Funerals: par. 19.

Reflection: "We're number one" is a chant that can be heard when the members of a baseball, football, basketball, or any other team make it to the top. "We're number one" indicates that all others are ranked below. All the other teams have been defeated. Only the un-defeated team can claim victory.

Before God raised Christ from the dead, death was number one. Before the resurrection, death defeated every human being who had ever lived, was living, and would live. However, Jesus singlehand-edly defeated death and triumphed over the grave. He became number one, swallowing up death and claiming the victory of im-perishability and immortality.

Christ shares his victory over death with us. Death never wins. Whatever is on the other side of the grave is the opposite of what we experience on this side of it. We experience our bodies as per-ishable. If we do not feed them, they die. If we do not clothe them, they suffer. If we do not shelter them, they begin to deteriorate. All of that perishability is transformed into imperishability in the vic-tory of the resurrection. With Christ there is no need for food, clothes, or shelter. Our life will be in a new dimension.

Likewise, on this side of the grave we experience mortality. All things die. The leaves of the trees turn brown and die. A dead bird or squirrel is found in the yard or killed on the street. The dog or cat which we watched over for ten years is found lifeless. Mortality is the fate of every thing. But Jesus the mortal has become Christ the immortal. There is no need for life as we have known it. Because of Christ's resurrection, we enter into a new plane of existence.

We have hope. The victory Christ won through his defeat of death has been shared with us. Through baptism, we were plunged into the mystery of his death and resurrection, his perishability and im-perishability, his mortality and immortality. God, who lives in us, will not let death defeat us. We will share the victory over death and claim first place with Christ.

Questions for Reflection: How have you most recently experienced perishability, mortality, death? How have you most recently experi-enced imperishability, immortality, life?

Prayer: Immortal God, you did not permit your Son to undergo the perishability of the grave. You raised him to a new and immortal life, giving him victory over death. Strengthen my hope in his vic-tory. Guide me from life through death to the gift of immortality through Jesus Christ the Lord. Amen.

Journal: In what ways have you honored the bodies of the deceased members of your family and friends? In what ways have you hon-ored the resting places of the deceased members of your family and friends? How do those actions demonstrate your hope in Christ's resurrection?

10. SEEN AND UNSEEN

Scripture: (2 Cor 4:14–5:1) . . . [W]e do not lose heart. Even though our outer nature is wasting away, our inner nature is being renewed day by day. For this slight momentary affliction is preparing us for an eternal weight of glory beyond all measure, because we look not at what can be seen but at what cannot be seen; for what can be seen is temporary, but what cannot be seen is eternal (4:16-18).

Order of Christian Funerals: par. 38.

Reflection: What we can see is not the total of reality. Although we often forget that fact, after a few moments of reflection we realize how true it is. We gaze out the window and see a tree in the yard. The dead outer bark covers the living inner reality. A squirrel scampers from one branch of the tree to another. We see dark and light shades of gray fur serving as a coat for unseen lungs, heart, brain, and other vital functioning organs. People lie in hospital beds suffering from cancer, AIDS, an accident, a heart attack. They are attached to tubes carrying water, food, air, blood to their body. We see their outer nature deteriorating. What we cannot see is the renewal taking place within.

The human body is temporary; it will not last forever. After seventy, eighty, ninety—maybe a hundred—years, it gradually falls apart. The brain cannot issue commands like it used to. The heart cannot pump as strongly as it used to do. The lungs are unable to fill with the same amount of oxygen as they once did. Joints wear out. Muscles slacken. The process of dying is seen in our outer nature.

With the eyes of faith, however, we see that what is taking place outside in no way resembles what God is doing inside of us. As we are gradually conformed in suffering to the cross of Jesus on the outside, we are also being prepared for the glory of the resurrection on the inside. We should be careful not to miss what we cannot see, the eternal, when we look at what we can see, the temporary. Reality is much more than what we can see—and that is where we should be focused.

Questions for Reflection: After choosing a relative or friend who has recently died, identify how the cross of Jesus was traced in suffering on the outside and how the glory of the resurrection was etched on the inside of the person. How did what you saw strengthen your faith in what you could not see?

Prayer: God of all that is seen and unseen, as my outer nature wastes away, renew my inner nature day by day. As you trace in me the cross of Jesus through my suffering, also reveal the glory of his resurrection. Give me greater hope that what is temporary will be transformed into what is eternal. Hear my prayer through Christ the Lord. Amen.

Journal: Stand in front of a mirror and look at yourself. What do you see wasting away? What can you not see that is being renewed?

11. FAITH-WALK

Scripture: (2 Cor 5:1, 6-10) . . . [W]e walk by faith, not by sight. Yes, we do have confidence, and we would rather be away from the body and at home with the Lord. So whether we are at home or away, we make it our aim to please him (5:7-9).

Order of Christian Funerals: par. 38.

Reflection: It is not uncommon for most people to take a walk from time to time, especially during the warmer seasons of the year. Individuals can be seen meandering on sidewalks or strolling through parks. Some people walk their dogs. Others take a few steps and admire a well-groomed lawn or a bed of flowers. Walking not only gives us exercise, it enables us to see the neighborhoods in which we live.

Walking by faith means that we make our lifetime pilgrimage with God as our guide. We trust that God will guide our steps and show us which roads we should take throughout our lives. Such faith is like keeping our eyes closed as we cross a busy intersection of streets. No matter how many streets we have to cross, we will always find our way home if we walk by faith. We have confidence that God will not let us wander away or get lost as we journey through life.

On the day that our funeral is celebrated, a Christian sign recalling our lifetime faith-walk can be placed on our coffin. The sign or signs should not be things of the secular world, such as postage stamps to indicate that we were a philatelist, or coins to signify that we were a numismatist, or books to say that we were a philologist, or ears of corn to show that we were a farmer, or a national flag to manifest our service to our country. The sign or signs we want on our coffins should indicate how we walked by faith throughout our lives.

Appropriate signs can include a Bible, if we read or studied it regularly; a Book of the Gospels, if we were a deacon, priest, or bishop entrusted with the task of preaching the good news; a cross to indicate that we saw in it the suffering and victory of Jesus; a book of prayers, if we used the book as a source of our prayer on a regular basis; a sign of Christ, Mary, or one of the saints, if we possessed such a religious sign. The point of placing Christian signs on our coffin is to show the living that our lifetime faith-walk was directed by God.

Also, the point is not to proliferate Christian signs. Already, we will have been sprinkled with water to remind the living of how we began walking by faith in baptism. Then, our coffin will be covered by a white pall, a remembrance of the white garment we received when we were baptized. The Easter candle, from which we received a smaller candle and were told to walk by faith in the light of Christ, will be placed near our coffin. All of those signs will signify that we walked by faith and not by sight.

Questions for Reflection: What signs have you seen used during funerals which you have recently attended? Make a list of them and, if you can, indicate what they signified.

Prayer: God of the journey, you guide my steps throughout my life as I make my way home to you. Give me the confidence to walk by faith and not by sight. Help me to please you in all things. I ask this through Jesus Christ the Lord. Amen.

Journal: What Christian sign or signs would you like to have placed on your coffin? Make a list and write a paragraph explaining what each represents in your lifetime faith-walk.

12. CREMATION

Scripture: (Phil 3:20-21) . . . [O]ur citizenship is in heaven, and it is from there that we are expecting a Savior, the Lord Jesus Christ. He will transform the body of our humiliation that it may be conformed to the body of his glory, by the power that also enables him to make all things subject to himself (3:20-21).

Order of Christian Funerals: par. 19.

Reflection: What are the choices we have for the final disposition of a Christian's body? Most people do not consider that there are choices until they are confronted with the death of a family member or a friend. And yet there are many choices that need to be made in the face of death.

The usual choice is burial below ground. A hole is dug in the earth, specifically six feet deep, into which the coffin is lowered. Entombment in a mausoleum, an above-ground building, is another possibility. The casket is placed into one of the many drawer-like slots and the door is sealed. Some people forego any type of burial and donate their bodies to science. The body is used by medical students for study in preparation for practicing medicine with the living.

Another choice of final disposition is cremation. At one time banned for some Christians, this option may be employed either before or after the funeral liturgy. If there is to be no viewing of the body, it may be cremated, reduced to ashes by burning, immediately following death. If there is to be a viewing, cremation can follow the funeral liturgy. No longer is it necessary to purchase an entire coffin for the viewing of the body which is to be cremated; the family can buy a liner for the coffin. The liner is burned, but the coffin can be used again. The cremains, the ashes of a human body, are usually buried.

Disposition of the body in one of the manners listed above demonstrates respect for the person who, while living, was a temple of God's dwelling. The person was created in the image and likeness of God, and so we treat the body with the respect becoming that likeness. While we honor the body of the deceased, we are also aware that God transforms the body into one like that of Christ, whom God raised from the dead. Not knowing of what a glorified body consists, nevertheless, we believe that God raises us—dust or ashes—from the dead.

Questions for Reflection: How have you honored the bodies of dead members of your family or your friends? Did you use prayer, song, flowers, water, incense, etc.?

Prayer: God of heaven and earth, through the death and resurrection of Jesus, your Son, you have made me a citizen of heaven from where I await the coming of the Lord. I believe that he will transform my body of dust and ashes into that of his glory. Make my life and death a prayer of praise to you: Father, Son, and Holy Spirit, one God, for ever and ever. Amen.

Journal: What are your wishes for the final disposition of your body? Why have you chosen that form of final disposition? How does it reflect your faith in the resurrection?

13. ASLEEP IN HOPE

Scripture: (1 Thess 4:13-18) . . . [W]e believe that Jesus died and rose again, even so, through Jesus, God will bring with him those who have died. For this we declare to you by the word of the Lord, that we who are alive, who are left until the coming of the Lord, will by no means precede those who have died. . . . [W]e who are alive, who are left, will be caught up in the clouds together with them to meet the Lord in the air; and so we will be with the Lord forever. Therefore encourage one another with these words (4:14-15, 17-18).

Order of Christian Funerals: par. 27.

Reflection: In the middle of the first century C.E., those who believed that Jesus of Nazareth was the Son of God whom God had raised from the dead and were waiting for him to come to rescue them from the worldly chaos in which they were living were wondering what would happen to those believers who had already died. About twenty years had passed since Christ had died and been raised by God. Hope for his return was beginning to wane. Furthermore, hope was being diminished as the first believers were falling asleep in death. The living wanted to know what would happen to the dead when Christ returned.

No one in the first century had asked such a question before because all followers of Jesus Christ presumed that they would be alive when he returned in a very short time. As days and months turned into years and the Lord did not come, the question demanded an answer. Paul, in the oldest of the New Testament writings—1 Thessalonians—offered consolation and hope to those who were on the verge of giving up their stance of waiting for the Lord's coming.

Using their faith in Christ's resurrection as his basis, Paul told the Thessalonians that it would make no difference if believers were dead or alive when the Lord returned. No one will have an advantage over anyone else, the apostle said. The God who raised Christ from the dead will raise all the dead and take them and the living to God's self when Christ returns. Paul pictures the "event" as a grand ascension of people, who inhabit the second story of the universe, to the first story where God lives. The members of the community who have died, those who inhabit the third story, will be raised, states Paul, and with the living will rise to be with the Lord for ever.

Just like Paul offered comfort and renewed hope to his first-century readers, during a funeral liturgy the homilist offers consolation and strength to those present to help them face the death of a member of their family or a friend. The question, what about those who have died, remains. The answer has to fit twentieth-century mourners whose generations of ancestors have waited for Christ's return for almost two thousand years.

Hope is shared by both the dead and the living. That hope is that what God did for Christ God will do for us. God does not renege on promises. Those who fall asleep in death do just that—they sleep. Consolation can be found in the daily experience of going to sleep and waking up. Just as we go to sleep every night and wake up every morning, so will the dead be awakened when the Lord comes. Their sleep is not eternal; it is temporary. One day the dead will be awakened by Christ and joined to the Lord forever. Such is our hope. Such is our faith. We wait for God to fulfill the promise. We encourage one another with our hope, our faith, and our patient waiting.

Questions for Reflection: How does your faith in the resurrection of Christ give you hope when you are faced with the death of a member of your family or a friend? What metaphors, such as sleeping and waking, do you use to communicate your hope to others?

Prayer: God of consolation, when your Son, Jesus Christ, fell asleep in death, you awakened him to the new life of the resurrection and promised that you would awaken all who fell asleep in his name. Enable me to encourage my brothers and sisters with the hope I share with them in Christ. May I fall asleep in hope and wake to share in eternal life. I ask this through Christ the Lord. Amen.

Journal: What questions do you have about death? Make a list of them. For each question, write an answer. How does your faith in God and your hope in the resurrection of Christ help you to answer your questions?

14. PASSOVER

Scripture: (2 Tim 2:8-13) Remember Jesus Christ, raised from the dead, a descendant of David . . . . The saying is sure:

> If we have died with him, we will also live with him;
> if we endure, we will also reign with him;
> if we deny him, he will also deny us;
> if we are faithless, he remains faithful—
> for he cannot deny himself (2:8, 11-13).

Order of Christian Funerals: par. 27.

Reflection: The paschal mystery of the Lord offers us the surety that what God did for Jesus God will do for us. Basically, the paschal mystery refers to the passing over of Jesus from death to life and the presence of God in his suffering, death, and resurrection. God, in the truth of the paschal mystery, is found where we would not have thought to look: in suffering, death, and resurrection.

God was present in Jesus' suffering. When we suffer because of a cold, cancer, or any other type of physical, spiritual, emotional, or psychological disease, God is revealing God's self to us through our suffering. God was present in Jesus' death on the cross. When we die, God's presence will be revealed through our death. And when we pass through death and break loose from death's bonds, we will discover God giving us new life.

Paschal first refers to the passover lamb, which was slaughtered and eaten in remembrance of the Israelites' escape from Egyptian slavery. With the blood of the lamb on their doorposts, God's people passed over from death to life. Jesus is the new passover lamb, who was slaughtered on the cross, freeing us from the slavery of sin. He passed over from death to life. Just as the passover lamb reminded the Israelites of the presence of God, the mystery of God's dealing with people, so, too, does the new passover lamb, Jesus, remind us of God's presence with us through every moment of our lives.

It is not God's faithfulness that is ever in question. It is our faithfulness. Sometimes, we deny God's work of the paschal mystery in our lives, but God cannot deny that God is always at work in us, guiding us through one passover to the next. We can be sure that if we endure our suffering and death with Christ, we will live and reign with him.

It is God's compassionate love that flashed forth from Christ's paschal mystery. It is God's compassionate love that is revealed in our paschal mystery.

Questions for Reflection: When have you most recently experienced the paschal mystery of another? When have you most recently experienced the paschal mystery in your life?

Prayer: God of Jesus, you revealed your presence in the suffering, death, and resurrection of Jesus, your Son. Open my eyes to see you in my suffering. Give me confidence to approach my death with the hope of seeing you face to face. Bring me to my passover from death to life with you and Jesus Christ the Lord. Amen.

Journal: In John's Gospel, Jesus is called the "Lamb of God." Based on the reflection above, what do you think are the meanings of such a reference? How does each meaning point toward the paschal mystery?

15. UNKNOWN FUTURE

Scripture: (1 John 3:1-2) . . . [W]hat we will be has not yet been revealed. What we do know is this: when [the Father] is revealed, we will be like him, for we will see him as he is (3:2).

Order of Christian Funerals: par. 236.

Reflection: We do not know what the future will bring. While it is true to say that the future is always breaking in upon us, as the present moment becomes past and what was future becomes present, we cannot know the future. We cannot know if we will be able to drive through the intersection without getting hit by another car until we have driven through it and emerged safely down the street. By the time we know it, however, the future has already become present and passed. Likewise, we cannot know that the plane will take off, fly to our destination, and land safely, until it has happened. Again, the future comes and passes too quickly. We cannot know if we will be alive in the next ten minutes. By the time we find out, what was a future ten-minute period has become present and passed.

When we celebrate the funeral of a child, we acknowledge that we do not know what the future would bring for the one who died at an early age. In the case of the death of a child, we come face to face with the uncertainty of the future. Our presumption that life lasts anywhere from sixty to a hundred years is questioned. We would presume that a child of a few years to the early teens would have a future of many years, yet death erases the future and quickly makes the present the past.

The inability to know what we will be, what God has in store for us, on the other side of death, is also a fact. We do not know what the future will be. In our terms of time, however, we can postulate that all time is eternally present for God. When God brings us to the present moment of future death, we will pass through it and discover the life that is always present with God. We will escape the limitations of time and, being like God, we will see God as God is.

When a child dies, we praise the God who gives all life and enables us to experience it as past, present, and future. We thank God for the love shown in creating children and adults, even as we wait to see into what the present will pass and what the unknown future will become in the present.

Questions for Reflection: What do you think you will be in the future? What do you think will be revealed to you on the other side of death?

Prayer: God of all time, past, present, and future are but one moment to you. Help me to recognize the signs of your presence in the past events of my life so that I might better recognize them now. Give me the confidence that in the future I will see you face to face. Hear this prayer through the Lord Jesus Christ, your Son, who lives and reigns eternally with you and the Holy Spirit, one God, for ever and ever. Amen.

Journal: When a child dies, for what do you think people mourn most? How does your inability to know the future make you both fearful of it and hopeful about it?

16. LOVE

Scripture: (1 John 3:14-16) We know that we have passed from death to life because we love one another. Whoever does not love abides in death. We know love by this, that [Christ] laid down his life for us— and we ought to lay down our lives for one another (3:14, 16).

Order of Christian Funerals: par. 29.

Reflection: Genuine love of one person by another sets the loved person free. Authentic love does not manipulate or try to control the other person in the hope of getting loved in return, achieving what one wants, or in any way influencing the other to be, do, or say anything that is not genuinely authentic. True love loves the other as he or she is and not how the lover wishes the beloved would be. Unconditional love is sincere and honest before the one loved. Those who love authentically are able, metaphorically, to stand naked in each other's presence without fear or shame or anxiety or lust and see only beauty, truth, honesty, and freedom.

Jesus loved all people genuinely. He freed those who were sick from their illnesses. He did not manipulate or exercise control over others. He simply loved them as they were and invited them to follow him. He called forth from his first followers sincerity and honesty. He died loving those who nailed him to the cross. Opening wide his arms, he stretched them around the world and, hanging naked on the cross, he set all people free to be full of beauty, truth, and love. Loving unto death is the supreme demonstration of genuine love.

Those who follow Jesus are called to the same authenticity. Love gives life. Jesus' love gave God's gracious life to every human being. God's love gave Jesus life beyond death. Our love for one another continues the sharing of life that Jesus lived. When we love genuinely, we experience death—death to selfishness, to pride, to manipulation, to control—and we pass to life—freedom, joy, hope, excitement.

The practice that we get loving in this life prepares us to pass from death to life and to continue loving. When we are able to love authentically, we get a fleeting experience of how God loves in perfect Trinity. The love we share with others on this side of the grave, God's love, will sustain us to the other side of death, where we will live in God's love for ever. The union of God and all people we call the communion of saints. It is a union bound by the cords of love. When we lay down our lives in love now in any manner, we can be sure that we are following in the footsteps of Jesus, whom God loved through death to a risen life. Also, we can be sure that we are loving in union with all those who have loved authentically before us.

Questions for Reflection: Whom have you loved or do you love authentically? What experiences of that love do you remember? What does each experience tell you about genuine love?

Prayer: God of love, after his death on the cross, you looked in love upon the crucified body of your Son, Jesus Christ, and you raised him to new life. Trace in me the lines of your love. Give me the willingness to lay down my life for others. One day guide me in my passover from death to eternal life in the love you share with your Son and the Holy Spirit for ever and ever. Amen.

Journal: What members of your family or friends have died whom you loved authentically? How did/does your love for them help you believe that they have passed from death to life?

17. WHITE GARMENT/PALL

Scripture: (Rev 14:13) . . . I [John] heard a voice from heaven saying, "Write this: Blessed are the dead who from now on die in the Lord." "Yes," says the Spirit, "they will rest from their labors, for their deeds follow them" (14:13).

Order of Christian Funerals: par. 38.

Reflection: Anyone who is baptized has the opportunity to die in Christ. Because baptism initiates people into the body of Christ, the Church, unless they have renounced their baptism and Christian faith, they die in Christ. According to the Book of Revelation, they are blessed, happy, to be congratulated. They have completed a lifetime pilgrimage and now look like Christ.

To indicate that a person has died in Christ, a pall is often placed on the coffin when the body is brought into the church for the first time. The pall is nothing other than one's white baptismal garment. After being plunged into the death-dealing waters, we were anointed, like Christ, with chrism oil and dressed in a white garment. We were told that we had been clothed in Christ. The garment is a sign of our Christian dignity, which we were told to bring unstained to the everlasting life of heaven.

Just as we were dressed in a white garment when we began eternal life, so when we die and pass over to eternal life, we are dressed again in a white garment. The pall represents the Christian dignity which we will, hopefully, have maintained throughout our lives and bring to eternal rest.

That white cloth of dignity represents our acts of justice: the times we treated every human being with equal respect, stood up for the oppressed, or fed the hungry; the times we visited the sick in hospitals, nursing homes, or their own homes; the moments we spent with those in prison; the times we clothed the naked; the periods we lived simply so that others could simply live or contributed to shelters for the homeless; and on and on. We will be set free from those labors only on the day that we die in the Lord and present our baptismal garment-pall, our Christian dignity, to God.

Questions for Reflection: In what ways do you enhance your Christian dignity by serving others' needs? In other words, how do you make your baptismal garment whiter? What seems to dirty your garment? What can you do about the stains?

Prayer: Blessed are you, God of life and death. Through the waters of baptism you clothe me in the white garment of Christian dignity and instruct me to serve the needs of others. Send your Holy Spirit to guide me in recognizing the dignity of all people. One day, when I die in Christ and rest from my labors, dress me in the garment of your love in heaven, where you live and reign for ever and ever. Amen.

Journal: How did the members of your family and friends who have died demonstrate the Christian dignity they received when they were baptized? How do they continue to demonstrate it now? What good deed did each one do that you want to imitate?

18. BOOK OF LIFE

Scripture: (Rev 20:11–21:1) . . . I [John] saw a great white throne and the one who sat on it; the earth and the heaven fled from his presence, and no place was found for them. And I saw the dead, great and small, standing before the throne, and books were opened. Also another book was opened, the book of life. And the dead were judged according to their works, as recorded in the books (20:11-12).

Order of Christian Funerals: par. 38.

Reflection: In the ancient world and before the advent of computers and cash registers, people kept records by writing them in a book. Some families still keep their history of births, weddings, and deaths written on blank pages in their Bible. Accountants recorded loans and payments in a book they called a ledger. Things of importance to people were recorded in a book—sometimes any book that had a few blank pages.

Writing-in-a-book is a metaphor used by the author of the Book of Revelation to signify that whatever people do in this life will follow them past death and into the next life. In the book their works are recorded. The day of death, the day that the one sitting on the white throne, God, opens the book, is compared to an accountant balancing the ledger. The measure of good works indicates life or death. If one's credits (good works) are greater than one's debits (sins), then eternal life is given. If one's debits are greater than one's credits, then eternal death is given. The author is not thinking of a physical book, of course, but attempting to communicate that what we do in this life matters for the next life.

We can be sure that God does not keep physical books for people, maintaining a page for every person and daily recording each one's good deeds and sins. God's interest is that we live according to the word of God as revealed in Jesus. Our fidelity to that word brings us to eternal life. As a sign that a loved one has lived according to God's word, a Book of Gospels or a Bible may be placed on the coffin during the funeral liturgy. A person who read the Bible regularly or studied it frequently would be honored with the Book on the coffin. Fidelity to the word of God would have been manifested in that person's life. Now, our loved one's name is recorded in God's book of life.

Certainly a person who was Christian in name only and showed no interest in the Bible should not have a Book of the Gospels or a Bible placed on the coffin. The sign must be authentic. Also, the living must be careful while honoring the body of the deceased to be sure that they do not judge. Only God, the one seated on the throne, judges the dead and determines life and death. Living in fidelity to God's word, we trust God's justice on the other side of death.

Questions for Reflection: If there were such a record, what would your page in God's book have recorded on it? What items would you like to erase?

Prayer: God who sits on the great white throne, you are the judge of the dead, both the great and the small. Keep me faithful to your word and bring me to eternal life with you. I ask this through Jesus Christ, your Son, who lives and reigns with you and the Holy Spirit, one God, for ever and ever. Amen.

Journal: Create a ledger page with two columns. Label one "credit" and one "debit." Record every good deed you do today in the credit column, and record every sin in the debit column. At the end of the day go over your page and ask: How faithful was I to God's word today?

19. THIRST

Scripture: (Rev 21:1-5a, 6b-7) . . . [T]he one who was seated on the throne said, "See, I am making all things new. To the thirsty I will give water as a gift from the spring of the water of life. Those who conquer will inherit these things, and I will be their God and they will be my children" (21:5a, 6b-7).

Order of Christian Funerals: par. 36.

Reflection: For a moment, think about how much water we drink in a day's time. Most likely we begin with a cup or two of coffee. By mid-morning we may be ready for a glass of milk. Lunchtime will find us drinking a can of soda or some juice. By mid-afternoon we are ready for a cup of tea. Before dinner, a glass of wine or some other type of drink may be had. We may keep lemonade or Kool-Aid in the refrigerator. All of our daily drinking does not include trips to the water fountain or trips to the kitchen sink from whose faucet flows cool, clear, clean water.

We thirst for water, a sign of God's life. Grace, God's self-communication to us, is like water: it flows everywhere. Just as physical water keeps us alive, so does God's grace keep us alive both in this life and in the life to come. The spring of the water of life is God, who floods us with divine life. In our thirst, all we need to do is drink.

Growing up in rural Missouri, I learned about water through a natural spring which flowed out of the surrounding hills. At one time there was a spring house built over part of the spring; it offered a place to keep milk and butter cool before refrigerators and electricity came to the area. The spring, never frozen in winter, was forbidden to me as a child, because my mother feared that I would fall into it and drown. Her concern, however, often went unheeded, as I would stop along the road after a warm spring day in school and lay face down on the rocks, stick out my head over the water, and suck up the forbidden, but refreshing, liquid. The spring water always tasted better than any other water.

That spring was the center of life for the people who lived up and down the road of that rural community before the drilling of private wells became common. It was a place for people to come with their buckets and ten-gallon cans to get water, to meet each other, and to talk to each other. It was a place for children to play, to stomp in the nearby always-damp-spot of mud. The old folks—now long dead—told stories about the spring. It was their center of life. In many ways, it was life.

Water is life. Water signifies divine life. It makes the earth new in the spring and summer. Floods of water, which at first seem destructive, end up constructing new relationships among people, fertile fields, better structures. God's grace washes us clean in baptism, flooding us with new life. It continues to make waves in our lives until it carries us through death to new life.

The thirst we have for God's water, eternal life, carries us through death to the other side of the grave. Our thirst can be quenched only at God's throne, the font of life-giving water. It is there that we will never thirst again.

Questions for Reflection: For what have you thirsted today? How did you quench your thirst? How does each of those experiences make you realize how thirsty you are for God's grace?

Prayer: God of the water of life, you alone can satisfy my thirst for your life. Give me the gift of drinking from the spring of eternal life. May I never cease to thirst for you until I stand before your throne made new. Hear my prayer through Jesus Christ the Lord. Amen.

Journal: What experiences have you had of God's grace flooding your life? Of what water of life did you drink? After the flood, how were you made new?

Responsorial Psalms

1. SHEPHERD

Scripture: (Ps 23)

> The Lord is my shepherd, I shall not want.
> He makes me lie down in green pastures;

he leads me beside still waters;
 he restores my soul.
He leads me in right paths
 for his name sake.

. . . .

Surely goodness and mercy shall follow me
 all the days of my life,
and I shall dwell in the house of the LORD
 my whole life long (23:1-3, 6).

Order of Christian Funerals: par. 146.

Reflection: The image of a shepherd has several dimensions which we should explore. In the Hebrew Bible (Old Testament) before the Israelites moved into cities, they were a nomadic people raising flocks of sheep and goats for food, clothing, and shelter. The shepherd was responsible daily for tending to the sheep—seeing that they were pastured, watered, and not lost. If a sheep was injured, the shepherd cared for it by pouring oil on its wounds and bandaging them. A newborn lamb may have been brought into the tent with the shepherd if its mother was not able to care for it immediately. One of the best-remembered shepherds is Moses, who, while pasturing the flock of his father-in-law, saw the burning bush that was not burned and received his call from God to serve as shepherd of the Israelites. Moses led the flock of Israel out of Egyptian slavery to freedom.

Once the people settled into cities, which could provide their basic necessities for life, shepherds become social outcasts. City-dwellers looked down on the shepherds who lived out in the fields with the sheep, who seldom bathed and smelled like sheep, and who, like thieves, pastured their sheep on the property of others. By the time the Christian Bible (New Testament) was written, shepherds were very poor and part of the marginalized of society.

The image of God as a shepherd comes from the time of the Hebrew Bible when shepherds received a positive press. Just as a shepherd watched over the flock of sheep, so God looked out for his people. Just as a shepherd led the flock to pasture and water, so God led people to food and drink in the desert and, ultimately, to the Promised Land. When they were about to be defeated, God protected the flock by raising up better leaders, such as King David, who led the Israelites in conquering their enemies.

By the time the Christian Bible was written, the attributes of shepherd were applied to Jesus, who associated with the outcasts of society. The irony in referring to him as a good shepherd is that by that time there was no such person as a good shepherd! All who took care of sheep were considered marginalized, like tax collectors, prostitutes, and lepers. Those are the people Jesus chose to shepherd, leading them to the water of life and refreshing their souls. He led them in God's ways and showed them the mercy God has for all people. He called each of them by name to enter into God's house of rest and peace.

By nature, sheep need a shepherd to keep them from wandering away, to lead them to food and water, to drive away predators. Basically, sheep are helpless. To compare people to sheep is an insult. When we realize that we are the sheep of God's pasture and that Jesus is our shepherd, we are being treated as if we are not capable of taking care of ourselves. And that's the point. We need God to shepherd us throughout our lives. We need God to shepherd us through death to life in God's house, the new Jerusalem, that awaits us on the other side of the grave.

Questions for Reflection: Who has served as a shepherd for you? How were you shepherded? How were you like a sheep?

Prayer: God, my shepherd, I do not want because you have led me to the green pastures of your grace and given me to drink of your life-giving Spirit. Help me to follow the voice of the Good Shepherd, who offers me goodness and mercy all the days of my life. Guide me to your dwelling place, the new Jerusalem, where I may live for ever with you, the Lord Jesus Christ, and the Holy Spirit, for ever and ever. Amen.

Journal: What images for God, other than shepherd, might be appropriate for use in this day and time? Write a psalm, similar to Psalm 23, based on one of your contemporary images.

2. GRIEF

Scripture: (Ps 25)

> Be mindful of your mercy, O LORD, and of your steadfast love,
>   for they have been from of old.
> Do not remember the sins of my youth or my transgressions;
>   according to your steadfast love remember me,
>   for your goodness' sake, O LORD!
> . . . .
> Relieve the troubles of my heart,
>   and bring me out of my distress.
> Consider my affliction and my trouble,
>   and forgive all my sins (25:6-7, 17-18).

Order of Christian Funerals: par. 25.

Reflection: Grief, a deep distress caused by bereavement, is felt by most people when they are confronted with the death of a family member or a friend. Such sorrow is a natural, human response to the loss of another human being through death. Grief is usually manifested externally through tears, sobbing, loud cries, reaching out to be held or hugged, lack of hunger for food and drink, contorted facial features, and bent-over shoulders. Internally, grief can be described as depression, heart-break, loneliness, aloneness, feeling crushed, isolation, and a lack of awareness of others.

During times of grief, especially when a person has died, what is needed is remembrance. We remember what our loved one's life represented to us. We remember all the good that person did. We remember how God's image was revealed through the person who has died. Such remembering will not remove grief, but it will ease its pain as we adjust to the loss.

During a time of grieving, we also ask God to remember us and to show us God's mercy and steadfast love. God's mercy signifies solidity, loyalty, dependability. When we feel unstable, betrayed, with no one to cling to, God remembers and kindly shows us mercy. God's steadfast love represents a mutual sentiment between God and us. Steadfast, unshakable love buoys us up during the times when we feel alone and unloved. God loves us unconditionally, and that love should be remembered during times of grief.

The psalms can help us express our grief, distress, affliction, troubles. The psalms can also help us to remember that God remembers us and shows us mercy and steadfast love. God's mercy and love can turn our grief into praise of God for the life of our loved one. God's mercy and love can turn our grief into praise of God for the eternal life that the deceased now enjoys and which we await.

Questions for Reflection: For whom have you recently grieved? How did you feel inside? How was your grief manifested outside?

Prayer: God of mercy and love, from of old you have remembered me and forgiven my sins. When I grieve the loss of a loved one through death, show me your mercy and steadfast love. Relieve my distress and troubled heart, and help me to remember your mercy and love, which never cease. One day may I praise you, the one God, Father, Son, and Holy Spirit, for ever and ever. Amen.

Journal: In what ways has God shown you mercy? In other words, how have you experienced God's mercy? In what ways has God shown

you steadfast love? Or how have you experienced God's steadfast
love in your life? Write a psalm of praise to God for those gifts.

3. EXPRESSION OF TRUST

Scripture: (Ps 27)

> The LORD is my light and my salvation;
>   whom shall I fear?
> The LORD is the stronghold of my life;
>   of whom shall I be afraid?
> . . . .
> Hear, O LORD, when I cry aloud,
>   be gracious to me and answer me!
> . . . .
> Your face, LORD, do I seek.
> Do not hide your face from me.
> . . . .
> I believe that I shall see the goodness of the LORD
>   in the land of the living.
> Wait for the LORD;
>   be strong, and let your heart take courage;
>   wait for the LORD! (27:1, 7, 8b-9a, 13-14).

Order of Christian Funerals: par. 25.

Reflection: When we hear the word "suffering," we usually think of
physical pain, because when we are in pain, we are suffering. The
common cold with a runny nose and watery eyes and sore throat is
painful, and we suffer. A person who has cancer may undergo surgery
and either radiation- or chemotherapy. Each of those experiences
is labeled as suffering. A heart attack is announced by streaks of
pain in the chest and arms and much suffering.

There is, of course, mental suffering, such as in memory loss.
Emotional suffering can be brought on by rejection, the unexpected
death of a child, spouse, or close friend. When we think that we have
lost our faith or have wandered into the desert of not being able to
pray, we suffer spiritually.

The psalms, written by human beings experiencing similar suffering and pain, can offer comfort. People who are suffering want
to know why they must endure the cold, attack the cancer with lethal
means, have open-heart surgery, not be able to remember, deal with
death, or undergo doubts of faith. The psalmist wanted answers to
the same questions and pleaded with God, who is gracious, to give

them. People who are suffering seek God's face and beg God not to hide from them.

The psalmist also expresses hope and trust in God. Hope is present in God's light and salvation. When it is light, there is nothing to fear. Just as God saved people in the past, we can remain confident that God will save us from whatever may harm us. God is the stronghold, the sustainer of life. There is no one that we need to fear. Hope, waiting for God to display goodness to us in this life, can sustain us when we prepare to cross into the next life through death's doors.

Our trust is in God's strength. No one is more powerful than God. Our courage to suffer through pain—no matter what kind—comes from God. Our courage to suffer through pain strengthens us to suffer through the pain of death to the life of light and salvation that God promises. With such hope and trust, all we can do is to wait for God to act, as people of every age and culture have done before us.

Questions for Reflection: When have you most recently experienced any type of suffering? How did God give you strength to live through it?

Prayer: God of light and salvation, I do not fear pain because you are the stronghold of my life. Help me to seek your face through all of life's suffering. Fill me with your goodness. Make me strong and give my heart courage to wait for you who live with your Son, the Lord Jesus Christ, and the Holy Spirit for ever and ever. Amen.

Journal: When have you waited for God to act? How did you see God's face? In other words, when have you experienced God's goodness? How do these experiences make you stronger and give you courage?

4. LONGING FOR GOD

Scripture: (Pss 42 and 43)

> As a deer longs for flowing streams,
>   so my soul longs for you, O God.
> My soul thirsts for God,
>   for the living God.
> When shall I come and behold
>   the face of God?
>
> . . . .
> O send out your light and your truth;
>   let them lead me;
> let them bring me to your holy hill
>   and to your dwelling.

> Then I will go to the altar of God,
>   to God my exceeding joy;
> and I will praise you with the harp,
>   O God, my God (42:1-2; 43:3-4).

Order of Christian Funerals: par. 25.

Reflection: First, we have the imagery of Psalm 42. A person's soul, that which makes one unique and which desires to see God, is compared to a deer's thirst for fresh streams of life-giving water. When hiking through the woods, frequently we can cross what are referred to as "game trails," paths made through the woods by deer, elk, or moose. Wild game usually follow the same trail to a water source, be it a small stream, a river, or a pond or lake. At dawn or dusk, the deer can be observed traveling the trail to the water, stopping, and drinking.

People are like deer. We thirst for God. We long to drink of God's water-source, which we usually call grace. Employing a different metaphor, our eyes hunger to see God's face. Grace gives us a taste of what God is like, but we will never be satisfied until we have crossed the threshold of death and drink with delight at the streams of God's unending life.

Second, we have the feeling of Psalms 42 and 43. Our response to having a minute part of our thirst quenched by God's grace is to desire more. Like the deer who drink but twice a day, when we get to the source of life, we want to luxuriate in it. We would like our eyes to be so wide open that the light of God's face blinds us. The psalms make us feel torn between two worlds—this and the next. Not knowing how to swim, we would risk the danger of drowning and jump into the bottomless lake of God's love, confident that our thirst would be satisfied and our hunger would be abated.

Third, we have the symbolism of Psalm 43. God's light and truth lead us to God's hill or mountain. A hill or mountain is a symbol of where God lives. The top of a mountain is as close to the world above, where God dwells in light, as we can get. In a three-storied universe, God lives above the dome of the sky, above the light. In fact, God created the light. People live on the middle story, the earth. And under the earth is where the dead live. Led by God's light, both the living and the dead ascend the mountain to be close to God.

Another sign of God is the altar. Usually made of unhewed stones, the altar represented God's presence among people. Moses sealed the covenant with Israel and God by sprinkling the blood of bulls on the people and the altar. The cross of Jesus is often referred to as the altar upon which he shed the blood of the new covenant. Going to God's altar implies approaching God.

The Psalms are prayed at the time of the death of relatives or friends to indicate that the deceased, like deer, have had their thirst for God's flowing streams of grace satisfied. Our loved ones now enjoy eternal light and see God face to face. They have climbed the last mountain and live with God on God's holy hill. The dead now stand around God's altar and worship eternally.

Questions for Reflection: What other imagery, feeling, and symbolism do you find in Psalms 42 and 43? How can that imagery, feeling, and symbolism help you deal with death?

Prayer: O God, my God, I praise you with the words of my lips and the songs of my heart. I thirst for you; give me the grace that quenches my thirst. I desire to see your face; give me the light that never fades. I approach your altar; give me the joy of being in your presence. Hear my prayer through Jesus Christ the Lord. Amen.

Journal: In dealing with death, what imagery, feeling, and symbolism do you find helpful? Make a list and record your thoughts about each.

5. SOUGHT BY GOD

Scripture: (Ps 63)

> O God, you are my God, I seek you,
>   my soul thirsts for you;
> my flesh faints for you,
>   as in a dry and weary land where there is no water.
> . . . .
> [Y]ou have been my help,
>   and in the shadow of your wings I sing for joy (63:1, 7).

Order of Christian Funerals: par. 139.

Reflection: Usually, when we think about looking for something, we presume that what we seek is lost. So, looking for car keys implies that they are not in their usual place on the hook by the door, on the table, or on the counter by the telephone answering machine. Searching for a birth certificate in a file cabinet means that the document is not in the folder marked "Birth Certificate" and has been filed in another folder. Sometimes, looking for what is lost simply implies that we forgot where we put it, such as an old photograph, a high school yearbook, or a college sweetheart memento.

When it comes to looking for God, however, our presumption—that the one for whom we seek is lost—does not apply. When it comes to seeking God, we are lost, and we need to be found by the one who created us and redeemed us. In our search for God, God finds us. Like the psalmist, we may say that we are seeking, thirsting, and pining for God, but the fact of the matter is, we are the lost, dry, weary land in need of God's graceful rain.

God always finds us when we are lost. That is why God is our surety in times of grief. Mourning the death of a family member or a friend can cause alienation. Those who are grieving have a tendency to withdraw from others and from God. They isolate themselves in their own small, walled-in world, which is like being in a desert. They need to be found, and God comes to find them. During such a time of trial, God is our source of trust and hope. When we grieve, God looks for us, finds us, and turns our mourning into praise. God waters our desert and transforms our grief into trust and hope.

We can compare being found by God to a mother hen searching for her chicks. Anyone who has ever been around a hen and her brood will remember how the chicks have a tendency to wander away as they search for bugs and worms to eat. When the mother hen senses that all of her brood are not present and accounted for, she begins to cluck loudly. The heads of her chicks pop up as they listen to her call. In an instant they run toward her and huddle under her spread wings. God is like that. When we grieve, God looks for us and calls us to be consoled with the hope of eternal life.

Questions for Reflection: When have you searched for God only to realize that God was looking for you? In what experiences of grieving has God found you, offering you trust and hope?

Prayer: God, you are my God. I seek you even as I am aware that you are seeking me. Help me to hear your call. Quench my thirst with your grace. Hide me in the shadow of your wings. Put into my mouth words of praise for you, Father, Son, and Holy Spirit, one God living in perfect Trinity, for ever and ever. Amen.

Journal: What metaphors, besides that of a mother hen looking for and calling to her chicks, can be used to describe God's activity of seeking and finding people?

6. RECONCILIATION

Scripture: (Ps 103)

> The LORD is merciful and gracious,
> slow to anger and abounding in steadfast love.

He will not always accuse,
  nor will he keep his anger forever.
He does not deal with us according to our sins,
  nor repay us according to our iniquities.
. . . .
As a father has compassion for his children,
  so the LORD has compassion for those who fear him.
For he knows how we were made;
  he remembers that we are dust (103:8-10, 13-14).

Order of Christian Funerals: par. 13.

Reflection: Either two close friends or a husband and wife have a strong disagreement about something and end up hurling words at each other, tossing screams across a room, or leaving the other's presence by banging a door. Later, after a period of cooling down, both regret the previous situation and seek the other's forgiveness. Both parties want to restore the relationship they had before the disagreement. Both seek reconciliation.

In some cases, people wait too long before they engage in the work of restoring a relationship. When one of the parties of the disagreement dies, the other is left without the opportunity to mend the relationship. Since one argument can lead to a multi-year feud, as in the case of a nasty divorce, a loss of money in a failed investment, or the revelation of a personal secret, the restoration of the relationship may never be accomplished. The person still living is left with the task of both seeking forgiveness from and offering forgiveness to the person who has died. Such a process will take more time than if the relationship had been restored while both people were alive.

Sometimes, the living need to be reconciled with each other, and the death of a family member or a friend sparks the fire of the reconciliation process. I once experienced this after the death of my "second mother," a very close friend of my family with whom I lived for six of my teenage years. When she died, some of the members of her family were not talking to other members. In fact, during the wake service the night before the funeral, they aligned themselves on opposite sides in the mortuary. During the funeral liturgy, they sat on opposite sides of the church. In the cemetery, they stood on opposite sides of the grave.

Later, I learned that the death of my "second mother" had enkindled the flame that got all of them back together again. Their anger with each other had been dissolved by one person's death.

They had experienced God's compassion, God's mercy and grace, God's steadfast love through the death of one of God's children. God, who forgives sins, had led them, through the rituals surrounding the death of a mutual loved one, to the shores of reconciliation.

It is amazing how God can use dust to get people back together again. God remembers that we are made of dust and that one day we will return to the dust from which we came. When we remember this at the death of a relative or friend, we can recall how important it is to be reconciled with those who share the same dust we do.

Questions for Reflection: With whom have you recently had a strong disagreement and sought reconciliation? In what ways do you think both of you benefitted from the experience of being reconciled? How was God active in the process of reconciliation?

Prayer: Gracious God, you created me from the dust of the earth and showered me with your mercy and grace. As you are slow to anger and abounding in steadfast love, make me more loving and willing to forgive. As you do not deal with me according to my sins or repay me according to my faults, help me to seek reconciliation with those whom I have sinned against or with those who have sinned against me before we return to the dust from which we came. I ask this through Jesus Christ the Lord. Amen.

Journal: With whom have you experienced a need for reconciliation after he or she died? What was the issue that needed to be resolved? How did you resolve it?

7. FAITH, REVELATION, REDEMPTION

Scripture: (Ps 116)

> I kept my faith, even when I said,
>   "I am greatly afflicted";
> I said in my consternation,
>   "Everyone is a liar."
> . . . .
> Precious in the sight of the LORD
>   is the death of his faithful ones.
> O LORD, I am your servant;
>   I am your servant, the child of your serving girl.
>   You have loosed my bonds (116:10-11, 15-16).

Order of Christian Funerals: par. 25.

Reflection: Faith, radical trust in God without any type of proof, is the platform from which a psalm is sung. In the midst of affliction caused by pain, distress, or suffering of any kind, we place our trust in God. We trust when we have no reason to trust. Faith, believing when there is no rational reason to believe, is the psalmist's presupposition.

A psalm also reveals an aspect of God to us. Revelation, meaning to draw back the curtain so that we can see, is God's way of disclosing the various dimensions of God as God exists in perfect Trinity. We experience revelation when we understand that God loves us, like a father loves his children; Jesus loves us, like siblings love each other enough to stand together for each other; and the Holy Spirit loves us, like the unseen bonds that unite us in a family.

When we join in singing a psalm, we also discover the note of redemption. We have been bought back, saved, rescued from the raging river carrying us away from God. Usually, a sacrifice of some type is required as a substitute for the one being redeemed. Jesus became our sacrifice. He redeemed us, plucking us from the water and giving us a second chance for life. The bonds of death that once tied us up have been cut loose. We have been set free to live for ever.

During the funeral of a relative or a friend, we can sing about how precious a gift death is when it takes place in God's sight. Jesus, our brother, did not rescue us from physical death. He showed us how to remain faithful through it. He died doing the will of his Father. If we die doing God's will, then we can be sure that God will smile upon us. We will remain full of faith as we pass through death to life. We will be confident that the One who has redeemed us through the death and resurrection of Christ will not abandon us. The Spirit will maintain our bond not only with each other, but also with God.

Questions for Reflection: In what ways have you experienced faith, revelation, and redemption when a relative or a friend died? How was God present in each of your experiences?

Prayer: God of life and death, you did not spare Jesus, your Son, from the grave, but on the third day you bestowed upon him the gift of eternal life. When I am afflicted, help me to keep faith. Show me your love and strengthen my trust in the redemption of Jesus Christ. Enable my death to be precious in your sight. Hear my prayer, Father, through your Son, in union with the Holy Spirit. You are one God, for ever and ever. Amen.

Journal: In what ways can you refer to death as "precious"? In what ways can you call yourself a "servant" of God? How do you think being a servant and perceiving death as precious are connected?

8. PROCESSION

Scripture: (Ps 122)

> I was glad when they said to me,
>   "Let us go to the house of the LORD!"
> Our feet are standing
>   within your gates, O Jerusalem.
> . . . .
> Pray for the peace of Jerusalem:
>   "May they prosper who love you.
> Peace be within your walls,
>   and security within your towers" (122:1-2, 6-7).

Order of Christian Funerals: par. 120.

Reflection: While it has become a cliche, it nevertheless contains a great truth: Life is a journey. At the moment of conception, when each one of us, who had not existed before, came to be, we began a journey whose end cannot be seen. As we grew in the womb of our mother, we prepared to make our first trip through the birth canal and, so to speak, place our feet upon the surface of the earth. Literally, the next step of our earth-tour was crawling and then walking from one spot to another.

Our traveling continued as we sat upon a tricycle and pedaled our way up and down the sidewalk. Once we had learned the fine art of balance, our quest continued on a bicycle. Our wandering was somewhat perfected the day we passed our driving tests and got a license that permitted us to roam all over the country.

There are, of course, other types of journeys. We travel through kindergarten to first grade and elementary school. From there we make our way through middle school, to high school, into college, and maybe on to a school that offers us post-graduate opportunities. We travel through relationships: friendships, first loves, serious dates, and lifetime commitments. We cruise the oceans of self-knowledge, identifying ourselves as a child of our parents, a teenager of independent means, a young adult who accepts both personal abilities and limitations, an adult who has a place in society, a senior adult who shares the wisdom of life with those who are not always ready to learn it.

With so much journeying, it is appropriate that after our death we continue the trip. From the mortuary or other place where we have been waked, a procession will be formed to take our bodies to the church where we will be greeted with the baptismal signs of water and a white garment. As this initial separation from family and friends takes place, we will be welcomed to the house of God, where we were nourished at the twin tables of word and sacrament. Those who mourn our deaths will honor us not only with their presence, but with sweet-smelling incense which will remind them that we have crossed from death to life.

As soon as the services are concluded in the church, those who mourn our passover will take us on the last stage of our journey in this life. The final separation, our last procession, takes place as those present are invited to take our bodies to their final place of rest, the place of committal. Our bodies will be lowered into the grave or slid into a tomb or turned into ashes in the crematorium. Our lifetime-journey will be ended, and we will be declared to be home with God. Our feet, so to speak, will be standing within the gates of the new Jerusalem, where everlasting peace exists.

What is on the other side of death? We do not know. If there is any continuity between this life and the next, we must hypothesize that there will be some type of procession or journey. Certainly, the God who enables us to journey from conception to death would not bring the procession to an end.

Questions for Reflection: How has your life been a journey? Make a list of what you consider to be the major steps along the way in terms of growing up, your academic life, your spiritual life, your relationships, etc. How was each major step a period of transition for you?

Prayer: God of the new Jerusalem, from the moment of conception you have set my feet on a journey to you. Guide my steps to your house, to the eternal city where your peace exists. Help me to walk with security until my final procession takes place and I pass over from death to life to be with you, Father, and the Lord Jesus Christ and the Holy Spirit in the eternal Jerusalem, for ever and ever. Amen.

Journal: In what ways have the processions in which you have participated with the bodies of family members and friends from the mortuary to the church and from the church to the place of committal helped you deal with being separated from the deceased? In other words, how have the two last journeys with a loved one helped you deal with the finality of death?

9. VOICE OF CHRIST

Scripture: (Ps 130)

> Out of the depths I cry to you, O LORD.
>   Lord, hear my voice!
> Let your ears be attentive
> to the voice of my supplications!
> . . . .
> I wait for the LORD, my soul waits,
>   and in his word I hope;
> my soul waits for the Lord
>   more than those who watch for the morning . . .
>   (130:1-2, 5-6b).

Order of Christian Funerals: par. 25.

Reflection: When faced with the death of a member of our family or a friend, we may discover that we are withdrawing into ourselves. From a psychological perspective that is a natural reaction. We pay less attention to what is going on around us and look closely at what is taking place within us as we attempt to deal with the reality of death. We can honestly say that we have entered the depths of who we are. Also, we have entered into the depths of the experience of death. A more current idiom would have us express ourselves by saying that we are in the pits.

Going into the depths means entering into the fullness of the experience of death. From our inside point of view we cry for help. We don't want to remain self-ostracized. We ask God to hear our voice and to help us deal with the reality and finality of death. Metaphorically referring to God as a person with ears, we plead that the Almighty will hear our prayer for help.

The prayer we make is not our prayer alone. As members of the body of Christ, when we pray, Christ prays in us, for us, and as us. We, the member of his body, ask God to help us. Our prayer is Christ's prayer, which gives us the assurance that God's ears are listening to what we need. We trust that God will listen to the Son and grant his request.

That trust in God is what enables us to wait in the depths. That trust is the word of hope we need as we make our way out of our interior isolation and begin to move toward the outside world again. The psalmist compares such confident waiting to waiting for the morning. If you have ever gotten out of bed before the first streaks of dawn appear in the eastern sky, you know the over-powering sensation the dawn brings. The light shatters the darkness. If there are clouds in the sky, the pink, gray, and purple hues announce the life of the new day. The sunrise confirms our hope that the last night is not the end, even as the resurrection of Christ enables us to trust that death is not the end of life.

Questions for Reflection: When have you recently experienced being in the depths? Whose voice did you hear? How did you trust the word you heard and wait for it to be fulfilled?

Prayer: God of the depths, when I am confronted with death, send your word of trust to me that I may be assured that you listen with heartfelt mercy. I place my hope in your word and I await the resurrection of the dead, like those who watch for the sunrise. Grant me the grace I need through Jesus Christ the Lord. Amen.

Journal: After looking through the Book of Psalms in your Bible, which psalm is your favorite? How does it help you to express your inner feelings? How does it help you to be the voice of Christ praying to God?

10. GOD LISTENS

Scripture: (Ps 143)

> Hear my prayer, O LORD;
>> give ear to my supplications in your faithfulness;
>> answer me in your righteousness.
> Do not enter into judgment with your servant,
>> for no one living is righteous before you.
>
> . . . .
> Answer me quickly, O LORD;
>> my spirit fails.
>
> . . . .
> Teach me to do your will,
>> for you are my God.
> Let your good spirit lead me on a level path (143:1-2, 7, 10).

Order of Christian Funerals: par. 25.

Reflection: As a human being like us, Jesus experienced both the anguish and the fear of death. Anguish refers to the pain, distress, sorrow, and anxiety of death. Most likely, the passage from Hebrews about Jesus learning obedience through suffering (Heb 5:7-9) is an indirect reference to the Synoptic Gospels' account of Jesus' agony in Gethsemane (cf. Mark 14:32-42; Matt 26:36-46; Luke 22:39-46).

There, in his distress, he prayed aloud to the Father that his cup of suffering might be taken away, but only if God wanted it that way. The author of Luke's Gospel tells us that he prayed on the Mount of Olives, that an angel appeared to strengthen him, and that his sweat became like drops of blood rolling off of him and falling to the ground. Such a prayer was like silent tears, his entreaty to the Father to deliver him from the cross if it were the Father's will.

Both the author of Mark's Gospel and the author of Matthew's Gospel portray Jesus as thinking that even God has abandoned or betrayed him on the cross. In other words, even Jesus feared death. His final words consist of "My God, my God, why have you forsaken me?" (Mark 15:34; Matt 27:46). Luke records his final words to be "Father, into your hands I commend my spirit" (23:46), focusing more on Jesus' trust of God. No matter what those last words were, the author of Hebrews understands Jesus' death on the cross as an act of obedience to God. Jesus did God's will. And by doing the will of God, he was made perfect through his suffering and death. Because of his obedience, God raised Jesus from the dead and made him the model and source of salvation for all who follow him.

When we feel or think that God has abandoned us at the time of the death of a member of our family or a friend, especially a sudden death caused by a heart attack or cancer or stroke, we can be assured that both the deceased and we are being made perfect through our suffering. Like Jesus, we beg God to hear us, knowing that we have no innate right to be heard since we cannot present ourselves as judged without guilt before God. In the presence of God no one of us is righteous; every one of us is guilty of some sin.

Our guilt, however, does not stop us from petitioning the One who alone can remove our guilt and answer our prayer. When our spirits fall, we can, like Jesus, ask God to teach us to do God's will, to be obedient, even if that means drinking from the cup of suffering. The anguish can lead us to the level path of a new life upon which we can look back and understand how God was forming us into the perfect people God wanted us to be. Every step we take now enables us to be prepared for the final step through death to the life that awaits us on the other side of the grave.

Questions for Reflection: When have you most recently experienced anguish and/or the fear of death? What prayer did you pray? How did God listen to you and answer your supplication?

Prayer: Compassionate God, you listen attentively to my supplications when my spirit fails. When I experience anguish and the fear of death, teach me to do your will, like you taught your Son, Jesus, to obey you. Lead me with the Holy Spirit through the suffering of this life to the joys of eternal life in the realm where you are one God, Father, Son, and Holy Spirit, for ever and ever. Amen.

Journal: How does knowing that Jesus was a human being like us, one who experienced anguish and the fear of death, help you live more fully? How can Jesus be for you a model of one who learned obedience to God through his suffering?

Gospel Readings

1. CONSOLATION

Scripture: (Matt 5:1-12a) When Jesus saw the crowds, he went up the mountain; and after he sat down, his disciples came to him. Then he began to speak, and taught them, saying: "Blessed are the poor in spirit, for theirs is the kingdom of heaven. Blessed are those who mourn, for they will be comforted. Blessed are the meek, for they will inherit the earth" (5:1-5).

Order of Christian Funerals: par. 9.

Reflection: When we speak about consolation at the time of the death of a family member or a friend, we are referring to the act of alleviating the grief or the sense of loss experienced by the living. Consolation is a ministry, a service rendered to those mourning the death of a loved one. It is a responsibility which is shared in a variety of ways by the members of the community of faith.

For example, relatives and friends console the grieving through their presence. Before final disposition of the deceased's body they may visit members of the person's family, spend time with them in the mortuary, help them prepare for the funeral, bring items of food for them to eat. They may console through telephone calls, cards, and letters. Sharing a story about the person who has died with the living is another aspect of the ministry of consolation.

The Christian community demonstrates consolation when the members gather for the vigil service. Through song, prayers, Scripture readings, and petitions, those who mourn are consoled. Believers show the importance of the dead individual to the community as they come together for the funeral liturgy. The body of the one who once actively joined with them in manifesting the Church to the world is honored with baptismal water, the baptismal garment, the baptismal candle, incense, and is commended to God.

Those who lead the various services associated with the funeral—the vigil, the funeral liturgy, the committal—console the mourners through their preparation for the various services and their reverence while conducting them. Instead of taking all the parts themselves, they enlist members of the family of the deceased to lead the songs, to proclaim the Scripture passages, to pray the petitions, to hold the water and incense, to place the pall on the coffin, to carry the body of the dead. They themselves come prepared with precious words to speak about how God was at work in the life of their loved one and how he or she was God's temple, a dwelling place for God on earth.

Together, all the members of the Christian community offer the consolation of Jesus. They help to alleviate the grief and sense of loss that accompanies a family member's or friend's death. When they do so, they live the beatitude found in Jesus' first sermon in Matthew's Gospel: "Blessed are those who mourn, for they will be comforted" (5:3). They discover that the consolation they offer identifies them as happy, congratulated, for they have entered life's battles and come out winning. They have done what Jesus did when he offered consolation to those who mourned.

Questions for Reflection: In what ways have you consoled the grieving? What physical things did you do? What spiritual things did you do? How have others consoled you?

Prayer: God of all consolation, your Son, Jesus, declared blessed those who mourn and promised that they would be comforted. Make me a minister of consolation. Help me to unite my grief to that of others through song and prayer to you. Send your Holy Spirit to unite the hearts of my community of faith. I ask this through Jesus Christ the Lord. Amen.

Journal: In what ways have you discovered that you were blessed because you consoled those who were mourning? In what ways have you declared others blessed who consoled you during a time of grief?

2. INFANT WISDOM

Scripture: (Matt 11:25-30) . . . Jesus said, "I thank you, Father, Lord of heaven and earth, because you have hidden these things from the wise and the intelligent and have revealed them to infants; yes, Father, for such was your gracious will" (11:25-26).

Order of Christian Funerals: par. 18.

Reflection: Anyone who has ever taken the time to read more than a few verses of Matthew's Gospel quickly discovers that a basic presupposition of the Jewish author is that God is in charge of everything. The God of Matthew's Good News directs the course of human events, sets the stage for specific acts, and reveals scenes that resolve a crisis with God "more present" at the end than at the beginning.

The God who is in charge of everything uses children to reveal truth. That is one of the Matthean ironies—those who cannot know truth because they are not yet educated are exactly the ones who have received the revelation of all truth: infants; those who are by society's definition powerless and without rights are those who have all the power and all the rights: infants. On the other hand, the learned and the clever are portrayed as dumb, powerless, and without rights, when, in fact, they were supposed to be smart, powerful, and in possession of all rights.

With Matthean irony in mind, the church conducts the funeral rites for both the baptized, the catechumens, and the non-baptized. Because people are called sons and daughters of God through immersion in the baptismal waters, they are entitled to a Christian funeral. Catechumens, those preparing for baptism, are also entitled to a Christian funeral because they intended to one day be united through baptism to the whole Church. Should catechumens die before they are baptized, the church considers their desire to be baptized enough. God was at work in the catechumen's life leading the person through the stages of initiation. What was not done physically—baptism—was done by God spiritually.

In the case of a child who dies before being baptized, the same understanding of intention applies. When a child is baptized, the parents of the child present the infant for baptism and declare to the church that they will raise the child in the practice of the faith. Parents of an infant who died before baptism but who intended to have their child baptized have a right to a Christian funeral for their infant. Again, the church relies upon God, who is in charge of everything, to supply whatever may be missing.

The Christian burial of a non-baptized infant reveals the love of God in a unique manner. God, who from the first moment of conception gives life, guides the course of that new life through its nine-month period of development and brings it forth from its mother's womb in the miracle of birth. In some cases, the newborn infant lives but a few minutes or hours or days. Through its funeral rites, the Church declares that God, who is all wise and intelligent, revealed divine love in the short life of the dead child. That love is shared by all and celebrated with the greatest of care by the whole Church.

Questions for Reflection: Have you participated in funerals for the baptized, catechumens, and infants who died before baptism? What did the funeral for the baptized, for the catechumen, and for the non-baptized infant reveal to you about God?

Prayer: God of heaven and earth, sometimes you hide your wisdom from the learned and the clever and reveal it to infants. You will that nothing you created should be lost, but that all should return to you, the source of all that is. Make me more aware of the love you show all people. Help me to recognize you in every person I meet. Hear my prayer through Jesus Christ the Lord. Amen.

Journal: Irony, by definition, is the use of words to express something other than and especially the opposite of the literal meaning. Choose a deceased member of your family or a friend and identify how God was revealing God's love in what first appeared to be anything but God's presence in the life of that person. In other words, identify the irony in the life of a loved one and indicate how God was there directing his or her life.

3. WISE OR FOOLISH

Scripture: (Matt 25:1-13) . . . [A]t midnight there was a shout, "Look! Here is the bridegroom! Come out to meet him." Then all those bridesmaids got up and trimmed their lamps. The foolish said to the wise, "Give us some of your oil, for our lamps are going out." But the wise replied, "No! there will not be enough for you and for us; you had better go to the dealers and buy some for yourselves." And while they went to buy it, the bridegroom came, and those who were ready went with him into the wedding banquet; and the door was shut (25:6-10).

Order of Christian Funerals: par. 41.

Reflection: The parable of the ten bridesmaids, unique to Matthew's Gospel, is an analogy exhorting the reader to be ready when the bridegroom comes. The bridegroom is Christ, who has returned to judge the nations and to lead the procession of those who have oil for their lamps into the wedding banquet, heaven. Before the bridegroom comes and the procession begins, the parable tells us to be sure that we have enough oil for our lamps.

Those who run out of oil are doubly foolish. First, they fail to be prepared for the bridegroom's return and wait with an insufficient supply of oil. Second, when the wise bridesmaids tell them to go to the dealers and buy some, the foolish ones run away from the approaching bridegroom instead of remaining there and at least hoping to sneak into the wedding banquet. When they return, the door is locked and they can't get in.

In Matthean terms, the foolish bridesmaids have no supply of the good works of taking care of those in need—oil. The author of Matthew's Gospel refers to caring for the needy as a higher righteousness; people do the right thing because it is the right thing to do. Without knowing it, the bridesmaids who have plenty of oil have recognized Christ in the hungry, the thirsty, the stranger, the naked, the sick, and the imprisoned. They did not wait until the last minute to check their supply of oil. Thus, when he comes, Christ declares them to be righteous, free from guilt. They will enter into the wedding banquet prepared for them by God from the beginning of the world. The foolish will discover that they cannot get in.

During the celebration of the funeral rites for a loved one, we focus on the hope that he or she has been led by the bridegroom in procession into the wedding banquet, heaven. We hope that his or her good works were in sufficient supply to keep the lamp burning until the wedding banquet was ready to begin. We dramatize this hope through the processions with the body of the deceased.

First, there is the procession from the mortuary to the church. Reverently, if there has been a viewing of the body, it is prepared for transport. Friends and relatives say their last good-byes, the coffin is sealed and placed into the hearse, and the procession to the church begins.

Second, once the body arrives at the church, there is a procession into the church for the funeral liturgy. The body of the loved one is greeted with baptismal water and clothed in a baptismal garment (pall) with the Easter candle burning nearby. He or she is prepared for the wedding banquet and brought into the church where he or she feasted at the table of the Lord, eating his body and drinking his blood.

Third, once the rites of farewell honor the body of the dead with incense, the procession is formed again. Christ crucified on his cross leads the way to the place of final committal, where the dead sleep and their lamps burn waiting for the bridegroom to come on the final day to lead them into the eternal wedding banquet.

Those who are wise have enough oil for their lamps. Those who are foolish spend their time begging for oil from those who cannot share it or looking for it while the groom arrives and locks the door.

Questions for Reflection: Would you characterize yourself as a wise bridesmaid or a foolish one? If you are wise, what supply of oil do you have? If foolish, what do you need to do in order to acquire oil?

Prayer: God of the wedding banquet, through the waters of baptism you have made me a member of your Church, the bride, who awaits the coming of your Son, the bridegroom. Guide me to those members of your people who are in need that I may share my resources with them. When the day of my death arrives, may I be found with plenty of oil for my lamp and ready to enter into your wedding banquet where you live and reign for ever and ever. Amen.

Journal: Call to mind a recent death of a member of your family or a friend. What supply of oil did that person have for his or her lamp? In other words, how do you think he or she was a wise bridesmaid?

4. WELCOMED (OPTION 1)

Scripture: (Matt 25:31-46) . . . [T]he king will say to those at his right hand, "Come, you that are blessed by my Father, inherit the kingdom prepared for you from the foundation of the world; for I was hungry and you gave me food, I was thirsty and you gave me something to drink, I was a stranger and you welcomed me, I was naked and you gave me clothing, I was sick and you took care of me, I was in prison and you visited me" (25:34-36).

Order of Christian Funerals: par. 131.

Reflection: When we are invited to the home of friends for dinner, we expect to be welcomed upon our arrival. We presume that after ringing the bell someone will open the door, invite us to come in, and welcome us with open arms. If we enter a large office building, we expect to find a receptionist who offers us some words of welcome, even if it is only a "May I help you?" Likewise, upon arriving at church on Sunday most parishioners have grown accustomed to the ministry of greeters, people of the parish who stand at the doors and welcome all who come to worship.

The first time that we were welcomed officially to the Church was on the day of baptism. The minister greeted us or our parents at the door, asked a few questions, and traced the sign of the cross on our foreheads as a sign of being welcomed, not only by the members of the Church, but also by Christ. Then, we were invited to come to the ambo where we listened to the word before being plunged into the death-dealing and life-giving waters of baptism.

Even though it is not always ritualized, if we were married in the Church or attended a recent wedding, both the bride and groom and their friends were welcomed by the minister at the door of the church. Then, the procession toward the altar began.

After we die, we will be brought to the church for the last time. At the entrance, we will be welcomed with water, just as we were welcomed on the day of our baptism. Instead of tracing the sign of the cross on our foreheads, a cross may be placed upon our coffin to indicate that we were faithful followers of Christ and that we share in his victory over sin and death. Once buried, most likely a cross will be erected over our grave or etched into our tombstone.

The author of Matthew's Gospel envisioned Christ's return in glory as a king coming home after being victorious in battle and conquering his enemies. His triumphal entry will provide the occasion not for us to welcome the king, but for him to welcome us into his realm. The battle was fought over death. Jesus died, but God raised Christ from the dead. By living righteously, doing what is right because it is the right thing to do, we unknowingly serve the king by meeting the needs of those who are hungry, thirsty, strangers, naked, sick, imprisoned. We will be called blessed, happy, congratulated, and welcomed into the realm God has prepared for us.

The gathering of relatives and friends in the church for the funeral liturgy and their welcoming of the body of the deceased is a sign of what God has done. Just as the community claims its own, so God claims those who have followed Christ faithfully. Just as the deceased was welcomed into the Church through baptism, so he or she is welcomed through death into God's reign. The one who was a member of the assembly of believers and worshipers in this life is declared to be a member of the assembly of believers and worshipers in the life of God's reign.

Questions for Reflection: Where have you been most welcomed? How were you welcomed? How did you feel? What were the signs used to welcome you?

Prayer: God of all blessedness, from the foundation of the world you have prepared your reign for those who follow your Son, Jesus. Make me righteous by enabling me to recognize the needs of others and serve them in the name of Christ. Prepare me to be welcomed by you through my death into the eternal life which you share with

Jesus Christ and the Holy Spirit. You are one God, for ever and ever. Amen.

Journal: After recalling a recent funeral which you attended, identify how the body of the deceased was welcomed into the church. Were you a part of the welcoming? How did the welcoming rites reflect the dead's baptism? How did the welcoming rites reflect the loved one's place in the community?

4. SERVICE (OPTION 2)

Scripture: (Matt 25:31-46) . . . [T]he righteous will answer [the king], "Lord, when was it that we saw you hungry and gave you food, or thirsty and gave you something to drink? And when was it that we saw you a stranger and welcomed you, or naked and gave you clothing? And when was it that we saw you sick or in prison and visited you?" And the king will answer them, "Truly I tell you, just as you did it to one of the least of these who are members of my family, you did it to me" (25:37-40).

Order of Christian Funerals: pars. 27, 61, 141.

Reflection: Service is work performed to help another person. We speak of service organizations, such as the Lions Club or the Rotary Club. Public shelters serve the needs of the homeless. Soup kitchens serve meals to those who have nothing to eat. Food pantries offer bags of groceries to those who cannot afford some of the necessities of life.

The author of Matthew's Gospel understands service to those in need as a demonstration of righteousness. A person does the right thing because it is the right thing to do. Those who are called righteous saw other human beings in need and served them. They didn't know it at the time—they didn't need to know it at the time—but when they served others, they served Christ. At the time of their judgment, they are told that the needy were members of Christ's family, his body. Thus, when the righteous served them, they served Christ and, in so doing, they served themselves since Christ is one body.

Studies and surveys indicate that young men and women offer some of their time in service to their communities. They engage in service projects for classes in school, whose teachers offer countless in-service opportunities. Youth volunteer to help the sick in hospitals, to work with children in shelters, to tutor in after-school programs, and to supervise games during camp sessions. Young men and women give countless hours of their time in various forms of service, some of which helps them to decide on a career and a course of study for the future.

During the vigil or funeral liturgy for a young man or woman, the homilist uses the youth's service as an example of how the person lived a Christian life. The teenager didn't have to know that it was Christ he or she was serving by helping others. Those declared to be righteous in Matthew's judgment story didn't recognize Christ in the needy. They served because it was the right thing to do. All people, no matter what their ages, are called to a life of Christian service because such a lifestyle is the right way to live. Later, we will discover that anyone we helped was Christ.

Questions for Reflection: In general, how are young men and women involved in service in your community? Specifically, in what service organizations or work are teenagers you know involved? What do you think motivates them?

Prayer: Saving God, I do your will when I serve those in need. Move me through your Spirit to offer more of my life in service to the hungry and the thirsty, the stranger and the naked, the sick and the imprisoned. Help me to do what is right by serving the members of the family of Christ, who lives and reigns with you for ever and ever. Amen.

Journal: Recall a young man or woman you have known who died. What service did that person give to the community? How does the youth's service and the message from Matthew's Gospel give you strength and hope?

5. SELF-KNOWLEDGE

Scripture: (Mark 15:33-39; 16:1-6 or 15:33-39) When it was noon, darkness came over the whole land until three in the afternoon. At three o'clock Jesus cried out with a loud voice . . . "My God, my God, why have you forsaken me?". . . . Then Jesus . . . breathed his last. . . . When the sabbath was over, Mary Magdalene and Mary the mother of James and Salome bought spices, so that they might go and anoint him. And very early on the first day of the week, when the sun had risen, they went to the tomb. . . . As they entered the tomb, they saw a young man, dressed in a white robe, sitting on the right side. . . . [H]e said to them ". . . [Y]ou are looking for Jesus of Nazareth, who was crucified. He has been raised; he is not here" (15:33-34, 37; 16:1-2, 5-6b).

Order of Christian Funerals: par. 30.

Reflection: There is a lot about ourselves that most of us would prefer not to know. And even if we do know some things about ourselves that we do not like, we prefer not to have to change them. So, we pretend that they do not exist and ignore our weaknesses and faults. However, such selective self-knowledge can be dangerous. By embracing our own darkness we can enter the light as better people. Put simply, when we are willing to know ourselves well, we can change. We call the dying to our old selves and rising to new selves the paschal mystery.

Self-knowledge brings darkness and despair. Mark's Gospel records Jesus' final words as an experience of abandonment. After he was arrested, all of his disciples abandoned him, except Peter, who later denied knowing him three times. In Mark's Gospel, Jesus dies without his followers or mother. His last line, "My God, my God, why have you forsaken me" (Mark 15:34), is his experience of thinking that even God abandoned him.

As we get to know ourselves by reflecting on our own experiences of living, we discover that we often feel abandoned. My spouse says something to a third party and it gets back to me. I think that my spouse has abandoned me. Children tell their parents, "I hate you," and it is easy to feel abandoned. Friends engage in a disagreement and both think they have been abandoned. From the depths of our darkness we cry and come to recognize that the self-knowledge we gained was good for us.

As we emerge from our darkness to the light of a new day, we recognize that a change is needed. Forgiveness needs to be offered and received. Our self-knowledge enables us, hopefully, not to repeat the mistake again. Clothed in the white robe of trust, love, and reconciliation, we pick up the pieces of our lives and move on. We have been raised from the dead.

Self-knowledge and living the paschal mystery come to an end only with physical death. Throughout our lives we are always in the process of learning more about ourselves, of plumbing our inner darkness and shattering it with light. The more we know who we are, the freer we are to follow Jesus, who felt abandoned by everyone, including God, yet had his dark tomb opened to the early morning sunrise. Our daily experiences of being raised are but a taste of what the fullness of life on the other side of the grave will be.

Questions for Reflection: What have you most recently learned about yourself. How did you suffer? How did you die? How did your rise to new life?

Prayer: My God, even though Jesus felt all alone, you did not abandon him as he hung in death's darkness on the cross. On the third day, you opened his tomb to the light of resurrection. Help me to live his paschal mystery through self-knowledge. From my darkness of despair lead me to new life and the peace of your reign, for ever and ever. Amen.

Journal: Take time to reflect on the experiences that you had yesterday or today. For each experience identify your resistance to change. Did you enter into any darkness? If so, what was it? Did you emerge into the light? How? What have you learned about yourself?

6. RESTORED (OPTION 1)

Scripture: (Luke 7:11-17) . . . [Jesus] went to a town called Nain. . . . As he approached the gate of the town, a man who had died was being carried out. He was his mother's only son, and she was a widow. . . . When the Lord saw her, he had compassion for her and said to her, "Do not weep." Then he came forward and touched the bier. . . . And he said, "Young man, I say to you, rise!" The dead man sat up and began to speak, and Jesus gave him to his mother (7:11-15).

Order of Christian Funerals: par. 10.

Reflection: "To restore" means "to give back." Some people restore furniture, giving back its original design or color. An old home is restored, meaning that its wall coverings, floors, and woodwork look like they did when it was built. Men like to restore old cars, giving back their inner decor and outer bodies.

The author of Luke's Gospel narrates a unique story about Jesus restoring the widow of Nain's son. Jesus touches the bier and awakens the widow's son. The Lord not only restores the young man to life, but he also gives him back to his mother.

Not only is the dead young man restored, but more importantly, his mother is restored. An equal emphasis needs to be placed on the woman. As a widow in a patriarchal society, she has no man to take care of her—other than her son. With his death, she is without rights, without power, without defense. In other words, she has no one to care for her. By restoring her son, Jesus also restores her. In a sense, he gives her back her life. The widow's powerlessness is transformed into power by Jesus.

The death of a relative or a friend renders the mourners powerless. They find it difficult to maintain the routine tasks of daily living, such as cooking, laundry, cleaning. Those who mourn are preoccupied with the task at hand—preparing the body of the deceased and themselves for visitation, prayer, liturgy, and final disposition. They need the support of others, like the widow needed Jesus' compassion, to get through the hectic few days surrounding the death of a loved one.

Members of the community can help in the restoration of the mourners through their words of faith and their acts of kindness. Their words of faith may express hope in the resurrection of the dead, such as the widow's son and Jesus' own new life. Acts of kindness may consist of preparing and delivering a meal, doing a load of laundry, cleaning the house, mowing the yard, or simply offering to do whatever needs to be done. Those kinds of words and deeds help to restore the mourners to the routines of daily living.

Questions for Reflection: What words of faith have you spoken recently to those mourning the death of a relative or friend? What acts of kindness have you done recently for those mourning the death of a relative or a friend? What restoration resulted from your words and deeds?

Prayer: God of death and life, your Son, Jesus Christ, restored the son of the widow of Nain to life and restored the widow to care within the community. Through the resurrection of Christ, inspire me to speak words of faith and to do acts of kindness for those who mourn. After I die, restore me to the life you share with your Son and the Holy Spirit, one God, for ever and ever. Amen.

Journal: Who are the "widows," the powerless people, in your life? How can you restore them? Will it take words of faith or acts of kindness or both to give them back the fullness of life?

6. YOUTH RESTORED (OPTION 2)

Scripture: (Luke 7:11-17) When the Lord saw [the widow], he had compassion for her and said to her, "Do not weep." Then he came forward and touched the bier, and the bearers stood still. And he said, "Young man, I say to you, rise!" The dead man sat up and began to speak, and Jesus gave him to his mother (7:13-15).

Order of Christian Funerals: par. 15.

Reflection: The unique story of the raising of the son of the widow of Nain in Luke's Gospel depicts Jesus as moved with compassion for the woman and her son. The story of the nameless widow, which most likely comes from the account of Elisha raising the son of the

Shunammite woman in 2 Kings 4:8-37, serves in Luke's Gospel to prefigure Mary, a widow whose son, Jesus, dies on the cross and is raised from the dead by God.

The author of Luke's Gospel focuses on the compassion Jesus feels for both the widow and her son. He feels the double powerlessness of the widow, who, without a husband or a son to care for her in the ancient world, was considered worthless. He sympathizes with her grief and her loss at the death of her son. Jesus empathizes with the impotence of the young man on the bier in the face of death.

When faced with the death of a young man or woman, the family needs the compassion of Jesus given through the members of the Christian community. The new life given to the widow's son is the hope that the members of Christ's body share for the teen or youth who has died. We show compassion by professing our faith that God restores youth with eternal life. We demonstrate our compassion by our presence at the vigil and funeral liturgy.

It is a painful experience for a family to inter a young man or woman, to see buried its hopes for the blossoming of the youth's potential. However, if they are able, members of the loved one's family can minister to the rest of the community during the funeral liturgy. By serving as readers, musicians, ushers, pallbearers, or special ministers of the Eucharist, they share their grief and enable others to share their compassion.

Although he was not a young man when he died, during a funeral for an uncle, I urged my aunt to serve as a special minister of the Eucharist, ministry she already shared in her parish. Not only was she touched by the compassion of those to whom she ministered, but the members of the community felt a special closeness to her and her grief as she offered them the blood of Christ. After the funeral, she spoke about how much support she felt during the liturgy.

On the other side of the grave, God restores us, young and old alike. Just like Jesus restored life to both the widow and her son, his widowed mother's only hope, and prefigured his own resurrection from the grave, God promises eternal life to all of us. Jesus' rising from the dead prefigures our own. One day God will say to us, "I say to you, rise!"

Questions for Reflection: In what ways have you experienced the compassion of Jesus during a funeral for a young man or woman? Did you give compassion or receive it? How was your life restored?

Prayer: Compassionate God, your Son, Jesus, had compassion for the widow of Nain and her son, and he restored both of them to life.

Dry my tears and help me to dry the tears of others. Make me a minister of the hope I share in being raised to new life with Christ, who is Lord for ever and ever. Amen.

Journal: Today, who are the widows who need to have their lives restored? Who are the sons of widows who need to have their lives restored? In what ways can you show compassion to them?

7. THIEF

Scripture: (Luke 12:35-40) [Jesus said to his disciples,] ". . . [K]now this: if the owner of the house had known at what hour the thief was coming, he would not have let his house be broken into. You also must be ready, for the Son of Man is coming at an unexpected hour" (12:38b-40).

Order of Christian Funerals: par. 17.

Reflection: Life is like an hourglass that gets turned upside down the day we are conceived (some would say the day we are born), and never gets turned again. The sands of our hours, days, months, and years slip through the narrow funnel until the last grain slides to the bottom and we die. Death is as inevitable as life, yet it is referred to as a thief. The hourglass of life-death leaves us stretched like a rubber band. On one end we know that life is not permanent, but on the other end we don't think that death will come today. So, we label our inability to know when that last sand will fall through the hourglass a thief.

A thief does not announce the time of arrival. While we may have thought that thieves came primarily during the night, modern thieves come to break into our homes at any time during the night or day. In fact, a lot of thievery takes place during the day while people are away from home and at work. But, alas, thieves do not telephone and say when they will arrive. Otherwise, we would be home, have the police notified, and be ready to apprehend the thief.

Such is our inability to know and the inevitability of death. Thus, while still alive, we may wish to consider making plans for our own death. Not only will taking care of our last rites give us a sense of being in control and make it easier for the mourners, but the planning can remind us of the unexpected hour of death and fill us with the hope that we share in Christ's resurrection.

What should be considered? We may want to think about whether we want an open or closed casket. We can determine what our final set of clothes will be. We can plan the vigil by choosing readings and hymns and including personal notes about what these mean to us. The funeral liturgy can be prepared in advance. Scripture passages, hymns, specific Christian signs to be placed on the coffin, and prayers can be chosen. We need to decide what type of final disposition we want: burial—above or below ground—or cremation. If we are to be buried in the earth, where should that be? Do we own a plot in a cemetery? If we wish our body to be placed in a mausoleum, do we have a place reserved for us?

By preparing for death, we also embrace our Christian hope of resurrection. We can shape the final rites surrounding our death in such a manner that they express our hope for eternal life. Just as the sands of our lives gave Christian witness, so does the arrival of the thief, the Son of Man, who embraces us with love and offers us a new birth and a new hourglass whose sands will never slip through.

Questions for Reflection: Have you planned the rites surrounding your death? If you haven't, why haven't you done so? What keeps you from making those plans? If you have, why have you done so? What prompted you to make those plans?

Prayer: God of all life, I cannot know the hour the thief will arrive, but I can prepare for the inevitability of death with the hope you have given to me through the resurrection of Jesus Christ, your Son. Help me to be ready to meet the Son of Man. At the unexpected hour, take me to the eternal life you share with him and the Holy Spirit, one God, for ever and ever. Amen.

Journal: Do you want an open or closed casket? What final set of clothes will you wear? What readings, hymns, and personal notes do you want for your vigil service? What Scripture passages, hymns, specific Christian signs to be placed on the coffin, and prayers do you want for your funeral liturgy? Do you want to be buried above or below ground or to be cremated? Do you own a cemetery plot or a space in a mausoleum?

8. VICTORY

Scripture: (Luke 23:33, 39-43) When they came to the place that is called The Skull, they crucified Jesus there with the criminals, one on his right and one on his left. . . . One of the criminals who were hanged there kept deriding him. . . . But the other rebuked him. . . . Then he said, "Jesus, remember me when you come into your kingdom." He replied, "Truly I tell you, today you will be with me in Paradise" (23:33, 39-40, 42-43).

Order of Christian Funerals: par. 31.

Reflection: The word "victory" is usually used when referring to the defeat of an enemy, such as in war, or when speaking about success in a struggle posing great difficulties, such as in a sporting event. In the religious world, Christ is credited with the victory over death. The enemy, death, was conquered once for all by the resurrection of Christ. God defeated death through Jesus and bestowed upon him the victory.

That latter understanding of victory is found uniquely in Luke's Gospel, which portrays Jesus as a martyr. In the passion narrative the author of Luke's Gospel portrays Pilate, Herod, one of the crucified thieves, and the centurion standing at the cross as declaring Jesus innocent of any crime. Before he dies, the Lukan Jesus shares his upcoming victory with the thief who requests to be remembered by promising him Paradise, another way to speak about victory.

Paradise, the state of being with God, is used by the author of Luke to refer to what God accomplished through the death and resurrection of Christ. The thief, promised Paradise, which is synonymous with the reign of God, because he acknowledges that he is guilty, is forgiven by the innocent martyr, Jesus.

The music surrounding the funeral of a family member or a friend should contain the hope of sharing in Christ's victory. To the living it should offer confidence that the deceased, like the thief, have entered into Paradise, where they are re-created by God and offered a share in God's life. Music also has the power to lift up the spirits of the mourners, causing them to stop and ponder their own deaths and their own hopes for eternal life. The support that the music gives to the words of the vigil and funeral liturgies can console those who mourn and elicit their own faith in the resurrection of Jesus.

In a manner of speaking, all of us are like the thief in Luke's Gospel. We are guilty sinners before the innocent martyr, Christ. We do not deserve the victory over death that Jesus' resurrection has offered to us. But by acknowledging our weakness, we allow Christ to offer us the gift of Paradise. As crucified thieves, we have little choice but to accept the Paradise so freely offered to us.

Questions for Reflection: What music best supports, consoles, and uplifts you at funerals? How does it help you understand that the dead now share in Christ's victory? How does it offer hope to you that one day you will share in Christ's victory?

Prayer: God of the crucified, when your Son was nailed to the cross between two thieves, you declared him innocent of any crime and, through his death, restored Paradise to those who follow him. Help me to be a good thief—to acknowledge my guilt and weakness and to accept the life you offer to me through Jesus Christ, who lives and reigns with you and the Holy Spirit, one God, for ever and ever. Amen.

Journal: How are you like the thief who asks to be remembered in Jesus' reign? Identify the ways in which you have heard Jesus promise Paradise to you.

9. SILENCE

Scripture: (Luke 23:44-46, 50, 52-53; 24:1-6a or 23:44-46, 50, 52-53) It was now about noon, and darkness came over the whole land until three in the afternoon, while the sun's light failed; and the curtain of the temple was torn in two. Then Jesus, crying with a loud voice, said, "Father, into your hands I commend my spirit." Having said this, he breathed his last. . . .

. . . [A] good and righteous man named Joseph . . . went to Pilate and asked for the body of Jesus. Then he took it down, wrapped it in a linen cloth, and laid it in a rock-hewn tomb where no one had ever been laid (23:44-46, 50, 52-53).

Order of Christian Funerals: par. 34.

Reflection: There is a silence which is so loud it can be heard. It is a silence that is not the mere absence of noise, but the deafening silence that follows the death of a family member or a friend. When viewing the body of the loved one and celebrating the funeral rites, the silence of finality is heard by those who pray.

Silence is heard through the author of Luke's Gospel. As he narrates Jesus' death, he depicts the silence of the earth. A solar eclipse has taken place, and the eerie shadows quiet all of creation to hear Jesus' final words. Likewise, the temple is bathed in silence. Its curtain is torn in two, signifying that God has left and is no longer there. The emptiness of God's dwelling on earth shouts through the silence.

Then there is the silence of Jesus' final words. In Luke's Gospel, those unique words are "Father, into your hands I commend my spirit." Unlike Mark's Gospel and Matthew's Gospel, which portray Jesus as saying, "My God, my God, why have you forsaken me?" the author of Luke's Gospel portrays Jesus as returning to God the spirit he received when he was conceived in his mother's womb. This is the author's way of preparing for Pentecost, the pouring out of the Spirit on all of creation, in the Acts of the Apostles. The silence follows Jesus' final words as he exhales his last breath and we are left waiting for new breath, the wind of God's Spirit, who will enliven all of creation.

Luke's Gospel also presents the silence surrounding Joseph of Arimathea. Quietly, he removes Jesus' dead body from the cross, wraps it in linen, and places it in a silent tomb. Then, just as he mysteriously appeared from nowhere in the Gospel, he disappears, never to be heard from again. Thus, there is a silence to Joseph.

Such awesome silence in Luke's Gospel declares the importance of silence during the celebration of the funeral rites. We need to be able to hear the silence in between the words that are spoken. After each reading from Scripture, we need stillness to contemplate what we have heard. After each prayer in the final commendation and farewell and at the committal, we need calm to plunge us into the mystery of life which we are celebrating. The punctuated quiet of the funeral rites can enable us to hear the silence of the dead person, who can speak volumes if we but listen.

Questions for Reflection: Describe silence. What is the most deafening silence you have ever heard? What is the most quiet silence you have ever heard?

Prayer: God of silence, you were not deaf to Jesus' death. On the third day you awakened him by blowing into him the breath of your Spirit. Come into the quiet places of my heart and help me to hear you in the tiny sounds of life and death. Give me confidence in the resurrection of Jesus Christ, who is Lord for ever and ever. Amen.

Journal: Think about a funeral that you have recently celebrated for a member of your family or a friend. What silences did you hear? What did each silence teach you about life and death?

10. BANQUET

Scripture: (Luke 24:13-35 or 24:13-16, 28-35) As [two disciples of Jesus] came near the village to which they were going, [Jesus] walked ahead as if he were going on. But they urged him strongly, saying, "Stay with us, because it is almost evening and the day is nearly over." So he went in to stay with them. When he was at the table with them, he took bread, blessed and broke it, and gave it to them. Then their eyes were opened, and they recognized him; and he vanished from their sight. . . . That same hour they got up and returned to Jerusalem; and they found the eleven and their companions gathered together. . . . Then they told . . . how he had been made known to them in the breaking of the bread (24:28-31, 33, 35).

Order of Christian Funerals: par. 131.

Reflection: When we celebrate an important occasion in our lives, food is usually involved. After the baptism of an adult or a child, a meal will be served by the family of the newly baptized or, if baptism is celebrated in a group, by the parish. Graduation from high school and college is often accompanied by a banquet, during which awards for academic achievement are given to outstanding students. Once a sports season is finished, a dinner is held and trophies are awarded to the best baseball, basketball, volleyball, track, and tennis players. Following a wedding or an ordination, a reception—another type of meal—concludes the festivities. Meals of one type or another mark birthdays and anniversaries, Christmas and Easter, or any kind of gathering of family or friends.

The unique story in Luke's Gospel about Cleopas and another unnamed disciple of Jesus walking to Emmaus is built around a meal. After the two meet the unrecognized Jesus on their seven-mile walk from Jerusalem to Emmaus, they sit down to share a simple meal together. When the stranger breaks the bread and then vanishes, they recognize the risen Lord. Of course, this meal has been preceded in Luke's Gospel by many stories of Jesus eating with people, such as tax collectors and sinners, not to mention the last supper he shared with his disciples, and the other stories that Jesus told about dinners and who should be invited to them.

The author of Luke's Gospel portrays Jesus as one who shares bread with outcasts and sinners in order to prepare for the story of the walk to Emmaus. According to Luke, followers of Jesus of Nazareth recognize him risen from the dead when they gather to eat. In the breaking of the bread they proclaim his resurrection and profess their faith in it. He is present in his risen state, and they recognize him.

Baptism prepares us for the Eucharist, for the celebration of the breaking of the bread and recognizing the risen Lord among us. That is why the rites of the funeral liturgy begin with baptism—sprinkling of water, clothing with a white pall, placing a cross on the casket, putting the coffin near the Easter candle. Then, the members of the community with whom the dead person celebrated the Eucharist join together for the last time with the body of the deceased in recognizing the Lord in the breaking of the bread. The eucharistic meal which was shared on earth becomes a sign of the banquet which the dead now shares in heaven.

The breaking of bread on earth and the recognition of the presence of the risen Lord is a sign of the eternal banquet shared by those who were faithful until their deaths. The meal shared by the living is fulfilled on the other side of the grave. The deceased, now raised like Christ to eternal life, eats eternally at his table and lives forever in his presence.

Questions for Reflection: What special meals have you recently shared in which you have recognized the presence of the risen Lord? What ordinary meals have you recently shared in which you have recognized the presence of the risen Lord?

Prayer: God of the eternal feast, for me throughout my walk on earth, you have spread the table of your Son, Jesus Christ, with the broken bread of his presence. May this banquet be but a taste of the risen life I hope to share for ever in your presence in heaven. I ask this through the Lord Jesus Christ, who lives and reigns with you and the Holy Spirit, one God, for ever and ever. Amen.

Journal: Remember a recently deceased member of your family or a friend. What meals do you recall sharing with that person? Identify the ways that you recognized the risen Lord's presence during those meals. In what ways do you think the deceased is still with you when you celebrate the Eucharist with the community of believers?

11. EXPRESSING FAITH

Scripture: (John 5:24-29) [Jesus said,] "Very truly, I tell you, anyone who hears my word and believes him who sent me has eternal life, and does not come under judgment, but has passed from death to life. Very truly, I tell you, the hour is coming, and is now here, when the dead will hear the voice of the Son of God, and those who hear will live" (5:24-25).

Order of Christian Funerals: par. 135.

Reflection: That for which we hope has already arrived according to the author of John's Gospel. Now, the dead have eternal life. Now, we have passed from death to life. Now, the dead live. In theology this is called realized eschatology, that is, the future has become present through the death and resurrection of Jesus. It is a future overflowing with life.

The author of John's Gospel portrays Jesus as the summation of all time—past, present, and future—because he is one with God. He is God from the beginning. In other words, because there is no linear time with God, what we call the past and future are always present. Access to this timeless presence is through hearing the word of Jesus and believing it.

Hearing the word cannot be separated from believing in God and Jesus. They are not two different acts. In the very activity of listening to what Jesus speaks, hearers profess their faith and have eternal life. The person who was dead before hearing the word and believing is now alive. That one has passed from death to life and already shares in eternal life.

During the funeral of a relative or a friend, the believers express their faith through prayer and song. Singing becomes a medium for professing faith in eternal life and in the resurrection of the dead. The focus on the quality of the processional or entrance song to express the faith of the living is for the purpose of gathering together the diverse members of the community into one voice professing one faith.

Through their song about their faith in eternal life and the resurrection of the dead, the members of the community also intensify the common bond they shared with the dead person, who was one with them in expressing faith. Thus, the prayer of the living becomes intercession for the dead. The eternal life shared before death continues to be shared after death by those who believe. The bonds that unite the community of believers are not broken by the death of its members. Both the living and the dead share in the eternal presence of God. Both the living and the dead have life now through the death and resurrection of the Son of God.

Questions for Reflection: What are your experiences of hearing and believing? How have you experienced eternal life now, in the present moment?

Prayer: Eternal God, with you there is no past or future, only the eternally present moment. Open my ears to hear the voice of your Son. Open my heart to believe his words. Open my life and death to the eternal life he shares with you. I ask this through the Lord Jesus Christ in the unity of your Holy Spirit, one God, for ever and ever. Amen.

Journal: During your most recent participation in a funeral liturgy, what songs were sung? How did the songs express the faith of the community in eternal life and the resurrection of the dead? How were the songs prayers of intercession for the dead?

12. DESTINY

Scripture: (John 6:37-40) [Jesus said,] ". . . [T]his is the will of him who sent me, that I should lose nothing of all that he has given me, but raise it up on the last day. This is indeed the will of my Father, that all who see the Son and believe in him may have eternal life; and I will raise them up on the last day" (6:39-40).

Order of Christian Funerals: par. 146.

Reflection: The author of John's Gospel portrays Jesus as positing two points of destiny, the predetermined course of events. First, there is the destiny, the will of God, that Jesus should lose nothing of what God gave him. Second, those who believe in the Son of God are destined for eternal life and resurrection on the last day.

Most of us don't think about fate. We live with the presupposition that our lives are controlled by us. So, last night, we made plans for today. If it is a weekday, we prepared ourselves for work by setting the alarm on the clock to wake up in time to shower, dress, eat breakfast, and drive to our place of employment. Then, we went to work on the assembly line, at our desk, or at some other station. After a mid-morning break, we stopped for thirty to sixty minutes to eat lunch, went back to the workplace, took an afternoon break, and then waited for the whistle, buzzer, or clock to indicate that another period of work was ended. We drove home, maybe stopping to shop for items of food, and, after taking care of several household chores, prepared dinner, watched a little TV, and went to bed, preparing for another similar day.

If it is a weekend, we may have slept a little later, but arose to a full schedule of things that needed to be done around the house: cleaning, laundry, shopping. Then, along with fixing meals, we may have scheduled some entertainment, such as seeing a movie, and, after going to church, engaged in some weekend sports, such as golf, tennis, or football.

In neither of these scenarios did we ever think that we were destined to do what we did. We figured that we were in control of our lives, calling the shots, making the plans, and executing the moves.

However, the fate of faith is never being lost and being offered eternal life and resurrection on the last day. God destines us for God's self through Jesus. In Johannine theology, our faith in the Son of God determines that we are not lost. God has found us and draws us to the Godhead through Jesus. Furthermore, in Johannine thought, our faith destines us for life without end beyond the grave with the promise of being raised up on the last day.

We affirm our destiny during the funeral liturgy when we, as a community of believers, sing our song of farewell for the deceased. In the face of the impending separation caused by death, we say farewell to the member of our family or friend with confidence that what awaits him or her is what also awaits all of us: eternal life and resurrection. As members of the same body, the same community, the same Christ, we are destined for God.

Questions for Reflection: As you look back over your life, what do you think God destined you to be and to do? How can you be sure? How do you feel about that destiny? How was God finding you?

Prayer: God of all, your will is that you lose nothing of all that you have created. Draw me closer to yourself. Send your Spirit to find me and to guide me to fulfill the plan you have prepared for me. Give me a stronger faith in my destiny to share eternal life with you, and, on the last day, raise me up to be in your presence forever. I ask this through Jesus Christ the Lord. Amen.

Journal: What plans have you made for the rest of your life? In what ways do you think your plans are also God's plans for you? In what ways have you been found by God? In what ways have you experienced sharing eternal life now? In what ways have you been raised up, tasting your destiny to be raised up on the last day?

13. LIVING FOOD

Scripture: (John 6:51-58) [Jesus said,] "I am the living bread that came down from heaven. Whoever eats of this bread will live forever; and the bread that I will give for the life of the world is my flesh. . . . [U]nless you eat the flesh of the Son of Man and drink his blood, you have no life in you. Those who eat my flesh and drink my blood have eternal life, and I will raise them up on the last day; for my flesh is true food and my blood is true drink" (6:51, 53-55).

Order of Christian Funerals: par. 154.

Reflection: Most likely you are familiar with these old questions: Do you eat to live, or do you live to eat? The first question presumes that food supports life. We need food and drink, or we will die. The second question focuses on living so that we can eat more and more food. The fact that many citizens of the United States are overweight and the lucrative industry of diet pills, fads, and programs reveal that many of us live to eat.

When we come face to face with John's Gospel, we must declare that we eat to live. We eat the body of the Son of Man and we drink his blood so that we will have eternal life. Just as physical food keeps us alive, so the spiritual food and drink of Christ keep us living forever. They are real food and drink that sustain life now and beyond the grave.

The eucharistic food of the body and blood of Christ is a taste on this side of the grave of the fullness of life that we will live on the other side of the grave. When we celebrate the funeral liturgy, the food and drink we share not only recall the passover of Jesus but the passover of the deceased. Jesus passed over from death to new life. Our loved one, who ate the body and drank the blood of Christ, has passed over from death to life. By eating Christ's body and drinking his blood, we join Christ in his passover. We share in Christ's passover now through our communion.

Because we are united with Christ, the head of his body, the church, we pass over from death to life, just like he did. The funeral liturgy is a celebration of the deceased's passover. The one who feasted regularly on the body and blood of Christ, who passed over from death to life, now has passed over from death to life. What happened to Jesus happens to those who believe in him. Christ's flesh and blood gives life to the world.

In Johannine theology, those who do not eat the body and drink the blood of Christ have no life, just like those who do not eat physical food die. Eucharistic food sustains us now and beyond the grave. Our deaths, like Christ's death, become a living sacrifice of praise. We offer to God all that we are in the eucharistic banquet, and God gives us through Christ all that God is. Thus, our praise of God for the deeds done in Christ's passover from death to life is also thanksgiving for the deed that God has done in the life of the dead person, raising him or her to new life. The passover of Christ has been etched upon the life and death and eternal life of the deceased.

When we share physical food together, we share people. When we pass food from one member to another around a table, we are also passing around the lives of those who are seated at the table. Physical food is a means of familial communion. Likewise, when we share the body and blood of Christ, we not only eat the body and blood of Christ, we also eat and drink of the lives of all of the members of the community of believers—those living and those dead. Our spiritual food and drink is a means of communion with divinity and humanity. We enable the unity of the whole church and nourish one another by eating the body and drinking the blood of Christ.

Questions for Reflection: Spiritually, do you eat to live, or do you live to eat? What food has God given to you recently? How did your eating it become a foretaste of what awaits you on the other side of the grave?

Prayer: God, who gives me all gifts, I hunger for the bread of life and the cup of eternal salvation. Give me the body and blood of Christ to sustain me through my passover from death to life. Raise me up on the last day to share in the eternal banquet you have prepared through Jesus Christ, your Son, who lives and reigns with you and the Holy Spirit, one God, for ever and ever. Amen.

Journal: Recall the recent funeral liturgy of a relative or a friend and the other rites and meals surrounding it. In what ways did you mark his or her passover from death to life? What role did meal-eating play? How does sharing food and drink imply sharing life with others? How does sharing spiritual food and drink imply sharing eternal life with others and Christ?

14. FOUR DAYS (OPTION 1)

Scripture: (John 11:17-27 or 11:21-27) When Jesus arrived, he found that Lazarus had already been in the tomb four days. . . . [M]any of the Jews had come to Martha and Mary to console them about their brother. When Martha heard that Jesus was coming, she went and met him, while Mary stayed at home. Martha said to Jesus, "Lord, if you had been here, my brother would not have died. But even now I know that God will give you whatever you ask of him" (11:17, 19-22).

Order of Christian Funerals: par. 147.

Reflection: In narrating a story, the author of John's Gospel usually presents minute details which are easily missed by the reader but which are important signs for understanding the full impact of the narrative. Such a detail is the mention of Lazarus' being in the tomb for four days before Jesus arrives. To us, four days simply means four, twenty-four-hour sequences. However, for the ancient world, four days past death meant that the person was undoubtedly dead. Some ancient peoples believed that it took three days for the spirit or the life-principle to depart from the body. By the time four days had elapsed, there was no doubt that the body and its spirit had separated.

John's Gospel presents Lazarus as being "very dead" by having him in the tomb for four days. His spirit has left his body, and the process of decay and the stench that ensues from mortality has begun. There is nothing that anyone can do for Lazarus. He is really dead.

And that's the stance mourners assume when confronted with the death of a family member or a friend. Once the authorities pronounce someone dead and an undertaker removes the body, embalms it, and prepares it for final disposition, there is nothing more that any of the living can do for the person, who is really dead. There is nothing that can be done except to turn to God, the author of life, which is what Christians do.

We call upon God's mercy. We implore God, the master of life and death, to show mercy to both the dead and the living, like the Johannine Jesus who went to the grave of Lazarus to console Martha and Mary. We ask God, who is greater than we are, not to permit death to have power over the living or the dead.

We commend our loved one into God's hands, since we recognize that we are powerless to do anything once death has arrived. Only the Creator has power beyond the grave. Like Martha placing her confidence in Jesus, we entrust the deceased and their future into the hands of the God of life.

Through our calling upon God's mercy and commending the dead to God's benevolent care, we affirm our faith in the resurrection. Martha affirmed her faith in Jesus in two ways. She said that if Jesus had been present, he would have healed Lazarus and prevented his death from occurring, and she said that she knows God will give Jesus whatever he asks. Martha stands empty handed before Christ. She has no proof that her brother, Lazarus, will be raised, but she does have faith. And in the face of death, standing before the sealed entrance of the tomb, she professes a faith in eternal life. Her professed faith before the tomb creates a contradiction, just like the calling forth of the four-days-in-the-tomb Lazarus by Jesus forms a contradiction. Faith stares death in the face and declares it to have no power over life!

Questions for Reflection: What statements of faith in the resurrection have you made recently when attending a funeral of a member of your family or a friend? How were the statements contradictions? In other words, how did you stare death in the face and declare it powerless over life?

Prayer: God of the living and the dead, death had no power over Lazarus even though he lay in the tomb for four days. Death had no power over your Son, Jesus, who lay in the tomb for three days. As I call upon your mercy and commend the deceased into your loving care, strengthen my faith in the resurrection of Christ. Do for me what you did for him, who lives and reigns with you and the Holy Spirit, one God, for ever and ever. Amen.

Journal: When standing before the death of a family member or a friend, what types of helplessness have you experienced? What types of hopefulness have you experienced? What is the source of your hope?

14. MINISTRY OF CONSOLATION (OPTION 2)

Scripture: (John 11:17-27 or 11:21-27) Jesus said to [Martha], "I am the resurrection and the life. Those who believe in me, even though they die, will live, and everyone who lives and believes in me will never die. Do you believe this?" She said to him, "Yes, Lord, I believe that you are the Messiah, the Son of God, the one coming into the world" (11:25-27).

Order of Christian Funerals: par. 9.

Reflection: The ministry of consolation is a service that the members of the Christian community offer to each other. At first, death seems to separate one from others, and, in a sense, that is true. However, the ministry of consolation reminds us that we are not alone. The shared ministry of consolation rallies us together. It does not drive us apart in the face of death.

A funeral is for the living. We do not attend a funeral merely to honor the deceased. We should have honored them before they died, when they could appreciate and accept the honoring of flowers and cards and kind words. After a person is dead, we join together in prayer and song to console the living. In other words, we minister to each other, attempting to help alleviate the grief and the sense of loss that we experience.

The members of the Christian community form a unity in faith and in consolation. Their faith enables them to deal with the inevitability of death honestly. That is not an easy thing to do in the death-denying culture in which we live. The dying seldom complete their lives at home. They are whisked away to hospitals or nursing homes, where it is more antiseptic to die. Once dead, makeup is applied to their faces to remove the pallor of death, hair is permed and combed for presentability, hands are folded, and glasses, if the deceased wore them, are placed on the nose so that the dead individual looks like he or she is taking a nap. From such pretending, we need to be liberated. When my maternal grandfather died, relatives and friends approached my grandmother and said, "He looks like he's sleeping." To everyone she said, "No, he is dead!" No denying death or pretending for her!

The ministry of consolation, which belongs to the whole Christian community, names the reality of death for what it is. It does not pretend or cover it up. However, it does offer the hope to the living that what God did for Jesus God will do for the dead and for the survivors: resurrection from the dead. The One who is the resurrection and the life teaches us to look at death and see life. We who live and believe in Christ do not die, even though we look like we are dead. We live for ever.

Questions for Reflection: In what ways have you experienced our death-denying culture? Did you offer consolation to the mourners by naming the reality of death or did you join others in pretending that death was not the end to this life?

Prayer: God of all consolation, before the tomb of his dead friend, Lazarus, Jesus faced the reality of death and promised Martha a future of life. Not only strengthen my faith in Christ's resurrection, but enable me to console those who mourn. Give me the hope of never dying eternally and sharing in the resurrection of the One who is life, Jesus Christ, who is Lord for ever and ever. Amen.

Journal: In what ways have you been a minister of consolation? In other words, how have you helped to alleviate the grief of those who mourn? To whom did you minister? How did your ministry join you more closely to those who were grieving?

15. JOURNEY OF LIFE

Scripture: (John 11:32-45) When Mary came where Jesus was and saw him, she knelt at his feet and said to him, "Lord, if you had been here, my brother would not have died." . . . Jesus . . . came to the tomb. It was a cave, and a stone was lying against it. . . . Jesus said . . . "Did I not tell you that if you believed, you would see the glory of God?" . . . When he had said this, he cried with a loud voice, "Lazarus, come out!" The dead man came out, his hands and feet bound with strips of cloth, and his face wrapped in a cloth. Jesus said . . . "Unbind him, and let him go" (11:32, 38, 40, 43-44).

Order of Christian Funerals: par. 42.

Reflection: The metaphor that compares life to a journey is more appropriate in our own time than it was for the early Christians in Rome. With our cars, buses, trains, and planes we travel more than any people before us, and we travel faster. The means of private and public transportation get people to and from work, to and from business deals, to and from vacations. We may spend more time traveling than any of our ancestors.

However, when it comes to our last trip, our last journey, a part of it will be on foot, like the days of old, before cars, buses, trains, and planes were ever invented. The coffin containing our body most likely will be carried out of the mortuary by pall bearers on foot and placed in a hearse for transportation to the church for our funeral liturgy. Once we arrive at the church, the pall bearers will lift us out of the hearse and carry us to the door. Once the funeral liturgy is over, they will carry us out of the church, put us back into the hearse, and, if burial is our final disposition, follow the hearse to the cemetery, where they will carry us on foot to the grave or tomb. There, our earthly journey of life will end, but our heavenly journey to the new Jerusalem, a metaphor for eternal life with God, has begun.

In John's Gospel, Lazarus was on a journey, one which Jesus interrupted in order to demonstrate the glory of God. Lazarus had been dead four days, but Jesus called him back to continue his journey. The point of the story, usually overlooked, is not the raising of Lazarus, but the journey of faith of those who surround his tomb. His sisters, Martha and Mary, journey to a deeper faith in Jesus. Many of the Jews come to believe that Jesus is the Messiah. In other words, there is more raising of the dead among the living than there is among the dead. Thus, the appropriate question is this: Who is really raised from death to life? And the answer is this: Martha, Mary, and the Jews are raised to life in faith, which will sustain them on their journey to eternal life. Lazarus is raised to life, too, but that is done in order to spark the faith of others, to display the glory of God.

As we read the story about Jesus, Mary, Martha, and Lazarus along our human journey, we hear the voice of Jesus calling us out of our tombs of disbelief into the light of faith in him. The response we give—either to stay buried in the dark or to emerge into the light of day and be unwrapped from all that binds us—influences how well we travel. Also, our final journey to the grave represents our hope for eternal life as we wait again to hear the voice of the One who called Lazarus to new life to call us to enter the heavenly Jerusalem.

Questions for Reflection: How do you think a recent funeral procession in which you participated mirrored the journey of human life of the deceased? What needed to be added to it or removed from it? Why?

Prayer: God of Martha, Mary, and Lazarus, I saw your glory revealed through the profession of Martha's and Mary's faith and the rebirth of Lazarus from the tomb. Give me a share in the faith of the two sisters. As I journey through life, help me to hear the voice of your Son, Jesus Christ, who calls me to the heavenly Jerusalem, where he lives and reigns with you and the Holy Spirit, one God, for ever and ever. Amen.

Journal: What metaphors other than "journey of life" help you to characterize your pilgrimage? What metaphors best help you to speak about your faith in the resurrection of Jesus and of those who believe in him? From what tombs do you need to be called forth?

16. GRAIN OF WHEAT

Scripture: (John 12:23-28 or 12:23-26) [Jesus said,] "The hour has come for the Son of Man to be glorified. Very truly, I tell you, unless a grain of wheat falls into the earth and dies, it remains just a single grain; but if it dies, it bears much fruit. Those who love their life lose it, and those who hate their life in this world will keep it for eternal life" (12:23-25).

Order of Christian Funerals: par. 9.

Reflection: Unless we live in Kansas, Colorado, or another wheat-growing state, many of us will most likely have never seen a grain of wheat. A wheat seed is straw-colored, tiny, and hard to see. It has a hard outer shell for protection, but inside it contains a potential plant. In order for the plant to grow, the seed must die. It has to be buried in the earth where the moisture can soften the outer shell and permit the plant to push itself up through the soil to the sun. The day the grain of wheat dies is also the day it comes to life.

One single of grain of wheat is placed into the earth, but as it grows and reaches maturity a whole head of grain is produced. When the harvest arrives, many golden grains appear. In effect, the grain of wheat has become a community of grains of wheat. Each individual seed has the potential to die and rise as a new community, or together they can be ground into flour, another type of dying, to be made into dough which rises into a loaf of bread.

When a member of the Christian community, a grain of wheat, dies, the others are called to support and strengthen the members of the dead person's family and friends through their faith in the resurrection. Each human life is like a grain of wheat. From the perspective of the world, every person is tiny and hard to see, yet everyone has a potential for eternal life deep inside. In order for new life to grow, we have to die, be buried, and rise. The day we die is the day we begin new life. While we are constantly engaged in this dying and rising, we need the support and strength of the other wheat seeds who form the head of grain, the community to which we belong. The lives and deaths of each seed enrich the lives and deaths of the rest of the grains of wheat.

Using the metaphor of "hour," the Johannine Jesus compares his own impending death to a grain of wheat. When his "hour" arrives, God's glory will be revealed through the Son's dying and rising. He falls into death and is buried in the earth, but he is raised and gives new life to all who believe in him. Jesus reveals the truth and the mystery that it is in losing life that we find its fullness. If we cling to life, we end up with only what we had. The grain of wheat cannot produce new fruit, new life, unless it dies. Neither can we!

When we participate in a funeral, we recognize not only the grain-of-wheat status of the deceased, but we name our own lives as grains of wheat. The death of the member of our Christian community is the culmination of years of dying and rising. One day, our death will be celebrated. Like a grain of wheat, we will fall into the earth and die. Hopefully, our death will give the hope for eternal life to those who remain. We believe that God will give the fullness of life to us on the other side of the grave.

Questions for Reflection: How is your life like a grain of wheat? Specifically, identify the deaths you have experienced and the new life that you discovered as you grew. To what can you compare your new life experiences after death?

Prayer: In your eyes, Almighty God, all of life is a journey of dying and rising. Help me to learn the lesson from the grain of wheat: only by falling into the earth and dying can I begin to live a new life. Never let me fail to strengthen those who mourn with my faith in the resurrection of your Son, Jesus Christ, who is Lord for ever and ever. Amen.

Journal: How do you think dying is like a birth? What of your hard, outer shell needs to be softened? How alive is the tiny plant deep inside of you? Does it yearn to grow? To what do you need to die now in order to grow into new life? What's keeping you from death and life?

17. WAY, TRUTH, LIFE

Scripture: (John 14:1-6) [Jesus said,] ". . . [Y]ou know the way to the place where I am going." Thomas said to him, "Lord, we do not know where you are going. How can we know the way?" Jesus said to him, "I am the way, and the truth, and the life. No one comes to the Father except through me" (14:4-6).

Order of Christian Funerals: par. 148.

Reflection: What we, the living, do on our side of the grave is meant to mirror what we believe God does for the dead on their side of the grave. Given particular emphasis is the final procession from the church to the place of committal. Since the deceased cannot walk there, the living carry the body to the cemetery, the mausoleum, the crypt, the columbarium, or wherever the final disposition is to take place. Thus, the dead is shown "the way." But there is more.

"The way" also refers to the faith of the dead during this life. They believed that Jesus not only showed the way to God, they believed that Jesus was the way to God. Through faith in the Son of God, we are united to the Father in a manner similar to the unity shared by the Father and the Son. Thus, Jesus is not just a guide to salvation; he is the source of salvation. The faith of the dead showed them the way through Jesus to God.

Also present in the life and death of the dead is truth. The source of all wisdom is God, who has shared it with Christ, who has revealed it to us. The basic truth is that God is one and has revealed the Godhead to us as three persons: Father, Son, and Spirit. United in love, the Father sent the Son to show us the way. In Johannine thought, the Son gave us the Spirit to guide us through life and death, to be the continued presence of Christ with us now, and to be our Advocate or Paraclete—lawyer—the one who pleads our case before God.

The result of knowing the way and the truth is life. Again, life does not mean mere earthly life, but sharing in the life of God, the life of the Father, Son, and Spirit. We share that life now through faith and will continue to share it beyond the grave. The final procession of the living with the dead mirrors the life that continues beyond. Simultaneously, the living walk with the dead through faith. They show the way in truth to the fullness of life.

In other words, the final procession is not just for the practical purpose of taking the body of the deceased to its final disposition. The final procession is itself a statement of faith. By walking in procession with the body of the dead person, the community declares that it believes Jesus is the way, the truth, and the life. Thus, what Jesus did while he was on earth—be the way, the truth, and the life—he continues to do through the Spirit at work in the individual believer and in the community of faith.

Questions for Reflection: In what ways is Jesus the way, the truth, and the life for you? To where have you been guided? What truth was revealed to you? How was your life enriched?

Prayer: Father of Jesus, you have shown me the way to eternal life through Christ, your Son, who revealed the truth of your love that sustains me through this life and into the next life. Continue to guide me with the Spirit that my faith may be proclaimed by the way I live and die. Hear my prayer through the Lord Jesus Christ, who is one with you, Father, and the Holy Spirit, for ever and ever. Amen.

Journal: Recall a recent funeral procession in which you participated. In what ways did the procession proclaim the belief that Jesus is the way, the truth, and the life. How did the unity of all processing with the body of the dead person strengthen your faith?

18. PRESENCE

Scripture: (John 17:24-26) [Jesus said,] "Father, I desire that those also, whom you have given me, may be with me where I am, to see my glory, which you have given me because you loved me before the foundation of the world. Righteous Father, the world does not know you, but I know you; and these know that you have sent me" (17:24-25).

Order of Christian Funerals: par. 150.

Reflection: There was a time in the past when the funeral liturgy was scheduled for early in the morning and the members of the Christian community would fill the church. However, with the lifestyle most of us live today, attending a weekday morning funeral is near to impossible without disrupting the whole day. Most adults barely have time to get up, eat breakfast, get the children ready and off to school, and get themselves to work without adding a funeral to the daily list of things that need to be done.

In some places, the funeral liturgy is scheduled for the evening hours when more people are free and able to attend. Because most places of committal close at the end of the work day, the final procession is scheduled for the next morning and, usually, only the relatives of the dead person participate in it. However, the presence of as many members of the Christian community at the funeral liturgy is meant to offset the latter reality. At least, scheduling the funeral for an evening offers the opportunity to the members of the community of faith to attend.

The issue is presence. Granted, people can be present through cards, letters, and flowers. However, bodily presence not only enhances the funeral liturgy, it also supports the family and friends of the dead and serves as an answer to the prayer Jesus is portrayed as praying in John's Gospel.

In the Fourth Gospel, Jesus is present to the Father from the beginning, before the world was created. Just as he is eternally present to the Father in love, along with the Spirit, so the Johannine Jesus prays that his followers will be present to him to share his glory. Such presence implies the faith of those who believe in Jesus. The world does not know him or believe, but those who do know and believe that the Father sent him are present to God by being present to him.

We share in Christ's presence, his glory, before the Father primarily by being present to one another. At the time of the death of a member of the Christian community, the presence of the living surrounding the body of the deceased declares that the dead individual is now present in the fullest sense to God, even as the members of the community are present to each other, mediating love and support. Presence begets presence and awareness of the unity all believers share in life and death through their faith in the Son of God.

Questions for Reflection: Whose funeral have you recently attended? How were you present to the other members of the Christian community? How were they present to you? How were you present to the deceased? How was he or she present to you? How were you present to God? How was God present to you?

Prayer: Righteous God, your Son, Jesus Christ, is eternally present to you and to me and the community of believers. When a member of my community dies, the prayer of presence is answered, as he or she sees the glory of your Godhead. Strengthen me with your presence through the Church, and enable me to be an instrument of disclosing your love to others. One day bring me to the fullness of life through Christ the Lord. Amen.

Journal: How do you think presence begets presence? Apply your answer to the Christian community. Apply your answer to yourself. What have you learned?

19. FINISHED

Scripture: (John 19:17-18, 25-30) . . . [C]arrying the cross by himself, [Jesus] went out to what is called The Place of the Skull, which in Hebrew is called Golgotha. There [the soldiers] crucified him, and with him two others, one on either side, with Jesus between them. . . . After this, when Jesus knew that all was now finished, he said (in order to fulfill the scripture), "I am thirsty." A jar full of sour wine was standing there. So they put a sponge full of the wine on a branch of hyssop and held it to his mouth. When Jesus had received the wine, he said, "It is finished." Then he bowed his head and gave up his spirit (19:17-18, 28-30).

Order of Christian Funerals: par. 150.

Reflection: The Jesus of John's Gospel, unlike his characterization in the Gospels of Mark, Matthew, and Luke, is in charge of his life, especially his passion and death. When Judas comes with the authorities to arrest him, Jesus tells them to take him after they bow down and worship him. Instead of the authorities and Pilate interrogating Jesus, he questions them. The Johannine Jesus carries the cross by himself; there is no Simon of Cyrene to help him. Before his death, he entrusts his mother into the care of the disciple whom he loved, and vice-versa. His last words, "It is finished," refer to the work he was given to do by the Father. The Johannine Jesus is even in charge of his death!

It is the fate of every human being to die some day. We don't have a choice. Oh, we might be able to prolong the day through medication, surgery, or therapy, but sooner or later each of us will have to say, "It is finished." Our life will come to an end, and we will die. We will cross over from life, through death, to life. This passover is called the paschal mystery. We will join the Lord in the life he shares with God on the other side of the grave.

Our active participation in the funerals of members of our Christian community is important for three reasons. First, we affirm the importance of praying for the deceased. Our prayer is not that an angry God will be merciful to the one who has died, but that God will help us understand that death does not separate us. The dead live a new life in a different dimension. They are still part of the communion of saints in which we share.

Second, our active participation in a funeral offers strength and support for the family members and friends of the dead person. Enthusiastic prayer and song has the ability to lift us up from our grieving. Without the support of the members of the community, those who are bereaved can slip into despair. The community gathers around them and offers them consolation and hope.

Third, when we actively participate in a funeral, we become a sign of faith and hope in the paschal mystery. Our faith declares that death is not the end. Life is changed, not ended. Like the Johannine Jesus, who declared his life finished and entrusted it into God's hands, trusting that God would raise him from the dead, we also bring our lives to the end and place them before the God who changes death into life. The paschal mystery is the passover of Jesus from death to life. It is God's revelation that what God did for Jesus—raise him to life—God will do for us. That is our hope for the future that cannot be seen.

On the day our life is finished, we will have the opportunity to profess our faith one last time as we entrust ourselves, through death, into the arms of the God who created us. Having been stripped of everything, including life, we will be able to cling to hope with the assuredness that what God did for Jesus, God will do for us.

Questions for Reflection: What recent funeral have you attended and actively participated in through prayer and song? In what way(s) did you affirm the value of praying for the dead, strengthen and support the bereaved, and become a sign of faith and hope in the paschal mystery?

Prayer: God of Jesus, at the end of his life, your Son, stripped of everything, gave himself to you in the hope of eternal life. As he passed through death, you raised him up in glory. I thirst for the fullness of life. Give me the faith of Jesus and the hope of one day having my thirst satisfied in the realm you share with the Lord Jesus Christ and the Holy Spirit, for ever and ever. Amen.

Journal: Think about the end of your life. How would you like for it to be finished? How would you like to be able to express your faith in the paschal mystery? What hope do you desire to take with you when you die?

16. Antiphons and Psalms

1. PS 23

See Part III: Texts of Sacred Scripture—13. Funerals for Adults, Responsorial Psalms, 1. Shepherd.

2. PS 25

See Part III: Texts of Sacred Scripture—13. Funerals for Adults, Responsorial Psalms, 2. Grief.

3. PS 42

See Part III: Texts of Sacred Scripture—13. Funerals for Adults, Responsorial Psalms, 4. Longing for God.

4. PS 51

See Part IV: Office for the Dead: Morning Prayer—First Psalm: Sorrow and Hope.

5. ROBED IN MAJESTY

Scripture: (Ps 93)

> The LORD is king, he is robed in majesty;
>   the LORD is robed, he is girded with strength.
> He has established the world; it shall never be moved;
>   your throne is established from of old;
>   you are from everlasting.
> The floods have lifted up, O LORD,
>   the floods have lifted up their voice;
>   the floods lift up their roaring (93:1-3).

Order of Christian Funerals: pars. 133 and 266.

Reflection: Psalm 93 portrays God as a king, dressed in a robe of fine purple with a sash of strength and sitting on a throne which is eternal. In a three-storied universe, God's throne is located above the waters above the firmament. Hence, the floods roar praise to God since the flood waters are closest to God.

In baptism we are robed in majesty. After the floods overwhelm us and we rise to new life with Christ, we are anointed with chrism as a priest, prophet, and royal leader and dressed in a white robe. We are told to bring our robe unstained to the throne of God in heaven. As a priest, we offer sacrifice to God. As a prophet, we call other people to conversion even as we are called. As royalty, we are robed in the life of Christ, which is nothing other than majestic splendor.

So, in death children, as well as adults, are welcomed into the church for the last time with the sprinkling of water in remembrance of the flood that once brought them death and new life. The coffin can be draped in a white pall. Thus, they wear in death what they wore in life—their baptismal garment. Those surrounding them in death declare that they continue to have life with Christ on the other side of the grave. They have been initiated into eternal life.

The death robe of majesty may be draped over the child's or the adult's coffin by family members, friends, or the minister who leads the funeral rites. Members of the community of faith dress the dead in white so that they, who have been clothed in Christ, may remember God's majesty and their own share in it through baptism in Christ Jesus.

Questions for Reflection: What are some contemporary signs of being clothed in majesty? In other words, what would designate royalty today—name plate on office door? sitting behind a huge desk?

Prayer: Royal God, you called me through the baptismal flood to new life. You anointed me with oil as a priest, prophet, and leader, as you called your Son, the Messiah, the Christ, the Anointed. Help me to live my Christian calling with dignity and bring my robe of majesty to the realm you share with the Lord Jesus Christ and the Holy Spirit, one God, for ever and ever. Amen.

Journal: How do you live as a priest, prophet, and leader? Indicate specific activities in your life that demonstrate each.

6. DIVIDED WATER

Scripture: (Pss 114 and 115:1-12)

> When Israel went out from Egypt,
>   the house of Jacob from a people of strange language,
> Judah became God's sanctuary,
>   Israel his dominion.
> The sea looked and fled;
>   Jordan turned back.
> The mountains skipped like rams,
>   the hills like lambs.
> Why is it, O sea, that you flee?
>   O Jordan, that you turn back?
> O mountains, that you skip like rams?
>   O hills, like lambs?

Tremble, O earth, at the presence of the LORD,
  at the presence of the God of Jacob,
who turns the rock into a pool of water,
  the flint into a spring of water (114:1-8).

Order of Christian Funerals: par. 133.

Reflection: The people of Israel have a history of crossing through water. After leaving Egypt, the nation approaches the Sea of Reeds; the sea divides and the people cross over. After forty years in the desert, they come to the Jordan River; it stops flowing and the people enter the Promised Land. The prophet Elijah rolls up his mantle and divides the Jordan so he can cross; Elisha, Elijah's successor, takes the mantle once Elijah has gone to heaven in a fiery chariot, strikes the river with it, and crosses over.

All of the water crossings form a sign of God's presence. God leads people through water. The divided water serves as a sign of a division in their lives. They leave one life behind and begin a new one. Their way of life is divided, like the water is split in two. God is with them as they make their way through the thresholds of their lives.

The God who divided seas and rivers for Israel continues to open up the waters today. The first time the waters are divided for us is baptism. We cross over from death to life. But baptism merely begins a lifetime of crossings. We pass through divided seas every time we change jobs, move from one home to another, change from being single to being married, traverse the crisis of disease to a cure. Whenever we become someone new in any way, by teaching, writing, formulating a new idea, for instance, we have crossed the river with God's hand leading and guiding us.

The last threshold we cross through divided waters is death. Water is sprinkled on our coffins at the threshold of the church, where we were once greeted and welcomed and immersed in the baptismal waters of new life. The water sprinkled upon us in death awakens all who believe to the new life we share across the river in the promised land of heaven. There, the hills skip in God's presence. Thus, just as our first acceptance into the Christian community was a threshold experience, so our last welcome is another crossing over divided waters.

Questions for Reflection: Make a list of five threshold, crossing over, life-changing experiences you have had. For each identify what type of water was divided. How have your threshold experiences made you a new person?

Prayer: God of Israel, you parted the seas and rivers so that your people could cross into a land flowing with milk and honey. When I crossed the waters of baptism, you gave me new life. Guide me with your Holy Spirit through the rivers of this life to the fullness of life in your presence. I ask this through Jesus Christ the Lord. Amen.

Journal: How has God caused new life to flow in and from you? Name specific experiences. What was old? What was new? How were you changed?

7. PS 116

See Part III: Texts of Sacred Scripture—13. Funerals for Adults, Responsorial Psalms, 7. Faith, Revelation, Redemption.

8. RECOUNTING DEEDS

Scripture: (Ps 118)

> O give thanks to the LORD, for he is good;
>   his steadfast love endures forever!
>
> . . . .
>
> Out of my distress I called on the LORD;
>   the LORD answered me and set me in a broad place.
>
> . . . .
>
> I shall not die, but I shall live,
>   and recount the deeds of the LORD.
>
> . . . .
>
> I thank you that you have answered me
>   and have become my salvation (118:1, 5, 17, 21).

Order of Christian Funerals: par. 141.

Reflection: As human beings, we have a tendency to forget just about everything, such as where we put grandmother's bowl, where we filed the important papers, where we left the car keys. Likewise, we tend to forget what God has done for us or just take God's mighty deeds for granted.

God, whose steadfast love lasts from before, through, and after time, not only does great deeds for people collectively—such as creation and the exodus—but for each one of us individually. Think about the last time you were in distress. Your discomfort may have been caused by a fender-bender accident in which no one was hurt; God worked a great deed and rescued you. Maybe you were diagnosed with an illness needing surgery; God healed you with a great deed through the hands of your doctor. An old relationship which ended because of a petty disagreement was reconciled; God did a mighty deed by inspiring the two of you to return to each other.

Even in the face of death, we praise God's mighty deeds, especially in the life of the deceased. We recall some of the works accomplished by God in the dead person's life. We remember how the paschal mystery of Jesus—suffering, death, and resurrection—was traced in the life of the dead. The focus of the homily during the funeral liturgy is on narrating how God rescues people—how God rescued the person who has died. The homilist stares death in the face and proclaims that we are not dead on the other side of the grave. We live and we recount the mighty deeds of God.

We recognize how little and helpless we are before God. Only God can do great deeds, for which we can only say, "Thank you." That is what we do at a funeral. We say thanks to God for God's work, God's presence flashing forth in the life of the deceased. The greatest deed of God, of course, was the paschal mystery of Jesus. Through Christ, God said that at those times we don't think that God is doing great deeds, like suffering and death, we are to look again. God is there rescuing us, raising us to life.

Questions for Reflection: What deeds has God worked in your life? How were you falling? How were you rescued?

Prayer: Saving God, you are good and your love for me never wavers. Countless times you have answered me when I called. You rescued me and gave me life. Make me grateful for all your works. May I praise you through your Son, the Lord Jesus Christ, and the Holy Spirit, for ever and ever. Amen.

Journal: Recall the recent death of a relative or a friend. What mighty deeds do you think God worked in his or her life?

9. INTERCESSIONS (OPTION 1)

Scripture: (Ps 119:25-32)

> [Lord,] my soul clings to the dust;
>   revive me according to your word.
> When I told of my ways, you answered me;
>   teach me your statutes.
> Make me understand the way of your precepts,
>   and I will meditate on your wondrous works.
>   . . . .
> I cling to your decrees, O Lord;
>   let me not be put to shame.

    I run the way of your commandments,
       for you enlarge my understanding (119:25-27, 31-32).

Order of Christian Funerals: par. 142.

Reflection: If we heard the cry, "Help!" we would respond with little or no hesitation. If we were near water, we would look for someone drowning. If on a hike in the woods, we would look for someone who was lost. If standing in a parking lot, we would look for someone harmed in some manner or locked out of his or her car. "Help!" evokes a response from us.

    So, we say to God, "Help!" in order to get God's response. Intercessory prayer is our call for help, saying to God that we cannot accomplish what needs to be done and that we are dependent upon God for assistance. Intercessory prayer is our acknowledgement that we are but dust. Making intercessions enables us to take ourselves less seriously than we usually do.

    We can cling to God's laws, precepts, decrees as guides for our life, but in the end, when all is said and done, we can only respond with "Help!" So, at a funeral, we respond to the word of God with our intercessions, petitions for the deceased and all who have died. We continue the dead's cry for help, asking that God forgive their weakness, sin, and raise them to new life. We pray for the bereaved and all who mourn, joining their cries for help to our own, and asking God to help them to understand God's ways and to run with God's commands. Intercessory prayer is made for all in the assembly. Together, all request help for each other to be more attuned to God's statutes.

    God, who is always faithful, hears our cries for help and saves us. We do well to reflect on God's help offered to us. We do better to accept it.

Questions for Reflection: When was the last time you asked God for help? What was your request? How were you helped by God?

Prayer: Merciful God, you know I am but dust in your sight. Give me the help I need to live according to the way of your commandments. Revive me according to your word and answer me. I ask this through the Lord Jesus Christ, your Son, who lives and reigns with you and the Holy Spirit, one God, for ever and ever. Amen.

Journal: Make a list of people you know who have died and those who are mourning their deaths. Write intercessions or petitions asking God to help them.

9. GIVE ME LIFE (OPTION 2)

Scripture: (Ps 119:153-160)

> Great is your mercy, O LORD;
>   give me life according to your justice.
>
> . . . .
>
> Consider how I love your precepts;
>   preserve my life according to your steadfast love (119:156, 159).

Order of Christian Funerals: par. 21.

Reflection: Psalms are songs or prayers on this side of the grave. Psalmists ask God to release them from their problems now. However, such a psalm as 119 is appropriate during the funeral for a teenager or a young adult. Those who pray the psalm stand on this side of the grave and ask God to grant the dead person life on the other side of the grave.

The prayer for life beyond death is represented, not only with words, but with signs. Teenagers and youth surround themselves with many signs of life. Music is signified by the person's collection of compact disks or cassette tapes. Clothes represent life, especially shorts and T-shirts. Photographs of the person with friends capture moments of life at parties, on field trips, and at school. Personal grooming products, earrings, and countless other items are signs of the life the teen or youth enjoyed.

While those signs represent earthly life and might be used in the funeral parlor during the vigil service to help those present understand who the loved one was, they are not appropriate during the funeral liturgy. The church has its own signs, and these point beyond this world to life beyond the grave.

The death and resurrection of Christ are represented by the Easter candle burning near the coffin, by the water sprinkled over the body of the dead, by the pall wrapping the loved one in eternal life. These baptismal signs simultaneously point back to the death and new life begun in baptism and the death and new life that await us on the other side of the grave.

The cross is a sign of Christ's death and resurrection, the establishment of the paschal mystery into which we are immersed on the day of baptism. The Book of Gospels or Bible, which may be placed on the coffin, especially if it is the dead's own, indicates how he or she tried to follow Jesus throughout his or her life. The incense, rising to the heights of heaven, honors the body of the dead and serves as a sign of the person rising to the fullness of life in God's presence.

The funeral of a teenager or a young man or woman is a time to celebrate life. The prayer of the community of believers is that God will give life beyond the grave in the same way God gave life on this side of it.

Questions for Reflection: What signs represent your life? Make a list of them and identify how each points to some aspect of your life.

Prayer: God of life, in your kindness you bring me to life and surround me with signs of your life-giving presence. I know that your love is everlasting. Sustain my faith and my hope in the life you promise beyond the grave. I place my trust in your justice through Jesus Christ who lives and reigns with you and the Holy Spirit, one God for ever and ever. Amen.

Journal: After your death, which signs of your life would you want used during your vigil service? What signs do you want used during your funeral liturgy (Easter candle, water, incense, pall, Bible, cross)?

10. PS 121

See Part IV: Office for the Dead—18. Evening Prayer, First Psalm: Keeper of Life.

11. PS 122

See Part III: Texts of Sacred Scripture—13. Funerals for Adults, Responsorial Psalms, 8. Procession.

12. HAND OF GOD

Scripture: (Ps 123)

> To you I lift up my eyes,
>   O you who are enthroned in the heavens!
> As the eyes of servants
>   look to the hand of their master,
> as the eyes of a maid
>   to the hand of her mistress,
> so our eyes look to the LORD our God,
>   until he has mercy upon us (123:1-2).

Order of Christian Funerals: pars. 28, 29.

Reflection: We take for granted our sense of sight, until we need glasses or contact lenses to focus clearly. We presume that we see the world bathed in light, until we suffer some type of trauma which leaves us temporarily blind. People who have cataracts removed can be heard talking about how, before the lenses of their eyes were replaced, they didn't realize how much they couldn't see.

The psalmist uses the metaphor of slaves looking to the hand of their master or mistress for food and mercy to depict the way we should look to God for all that we need. Our eyes should be focused on God, from whom all blessings flow. In the ancient world, the master's or mistress' hand was considered a source of blessing for the slave or maid. They received a daily portion of sustenance from their owner. Likewise, how the slave or maid was treated by the master or mistress was associated with the hand, since it could either gently console or violently slap the slave or maid.

Certainly, the psalmist does not imagine us to be slaves of God in the sense of being owned by God, but the song is meant to make us realize it is from the hand of God that we receive everything. We are dependent upon God for all that we have and all that we are. From God's hand comes life itself.

During the vigil and funeral liturgy for a loved one, the presider calls upon God's mercy for the dead and for the living on behalf of the whole Church. The intercessory prayers petition God to open God's hand and to provide for the needs of the dead, the family, other mourners, and all those gathered together in prayer. Using the metaphor of the psalm, we take the position of slaves and maids and look to God's hand to satisfy us. We pray that God will give us all that we need, especially during the time of the vigil, funeral, and final committal of our loved one.

Using the image of a three-storied universe in which God lives on the top level, we lift up our eyes to the God we cannot see. Our inability to see God turns us to use words of prayer. Knowing that we cannot raise the dead to life, we place our trust in God, believing that what God did for Jesus—raise him from the dead—God will do for our loved one and for us. From God's hand we receive abundant life now. From God's hand we believe we will receive eternal life.

Questions for Reflection: From whose hand have you received blessings? Make a list of people who have nurtured your life and for each person indicate what gift came from that person's hand.

Prayer: God of abundant life, I lift up my eyes to you in my need. I thank you for the many gifts you have given to me in the past. Show me your mercy and open wide your hand in blessing. I look to you for life now and in eternity. Pour out on me your Holy Spirit and hear my prayer in the name of Jesus Christ the Lord. Amen.

Journal: Make a list of several people in your family who have died. For each identify what blessings you think the person received from God's hand. How were the person's gifts shared with the community of believers?

13. RESTORED FORTUNES

Scripture: (Ps 126)

> When the LORD restored the fortunes of Zion,
> we were like those who dream.
>
> . . . .
>
> The LORD has done great things for us,
> and we rejoiced.
> Restore our fortunes, O LORD,
> like the watercourses in the Negeb.
> May those who sow in tears
> reap with shouts of joy.
> Those who go out weeping,
> bearing the seed for sowing,
> shall come home with shouts of joy,
> carrying their sheaves (126:1, 3-6).

Order of Christian Funerals: par. 147.

Reflection: When we hear about fortune, we think of great wealth manifested in a large bank account, lots of real estate, a multi-million-dollar home, a portfolio of the best stocks and bonds. Since such fortune seems to indicate success in the eyes of the world, we can spend our lives building up such a fortune and die with or without a designated heir to our wealth.

The psalmist sings about another type of fortune, the fortune of Zion, which refers to people, specifically to Israel (Jews), returning to Jerusalem after about seventy years in exile. The wealth of the city was not measured in dollars and cents, but according to the great things God did, rescuing Israel from Egyptian slavery and saving Israel from Babylonian-turned-Persian captivity.

The psalmist acknowledges the nation's total dependence upon God by asking for an abundant harvest to feed the people and the joy of freedom instead of the weeping of slavery. Such dependency, such reliance upon God, is a pure gift. All the people can do is rejoice.

When a member of the family or a friend dies, our focus should be on the spiritual life-long fortune, not the wealth measured in stocks and bonds and real estate and marked by dollar signs. Our spiritual fortune is found in recognizing our dependence on God for everything.

One way to focus on spiritual wealth is through silence during the funeral rites. Ample silence permits the words of Christian hope in God's abundant mercy to crack open within us. Silence in between the spoken words reminds us of God's promise of eternal life—a fortune beyond anything we could even begin to amass on this side of the grave.

We can go out into life sowing the seed of God's mercy and promise and come back to God carrying the harvested sheaves of good works and prayerful relationships. The God who restored Israel's fortunes promises to restore us to life on the other side of death. We await our inheritance.

Questions for Reflection: What do you consider to be your physical fortune? What do you consider to be your spiritual fortune? Which is more important to you now?

Prayer: God of Zion, when your Son, Jesus Christ, hung in death on the cross, you restored him to the fullness of life by raising him to eternal life. Change my tears to rejoicing. Create a harvest of joy from my life. Make me rich in your ways. I ask this through your Son, Jesus Christ, with the help of the Holy Spirit, who lives for ever and ever. Amen.

Journal: Recall the recent death of a relative or a friend. Of what did his or her spiritual fortune consist? How did the person share his or her spiritual fortune with you? with others?

14. PS 130

See Part III: Texts of Sacred Scripture—13. Funerals for Adults, Responsorial Psalms, 9. Voice of Christ, and Part IV: Office for the Dead—18. Evening Prayer, Second Psalm: Intercessor.

15. DON'T TURN AWAY

Scripture: (Ps 132)

> O LORD, remember in David's favor
>   all the hardships he endured;
> how he swore to the LORD
>   and vowed to the Mighty One of Jacob
>
> . . . .
>
> Rise up, O LORD, and go to your resting place,
>   you and the ark of your might.

. . . .
For your servant David's sake
  do not turn away the face of your anointed one (132:1-2, 8, 10).

Order of Christian Funerals: par. 11.

Reflection: There are two aspects of not turning away. First, the psalmist asks God not to turn away from King David. In the psalm, David becomes an advertising image, the epitome of kingship, a shepherd boy chosen by God to lead the tribes of Israel into a unified nation. David establishes peace, secures Israel's borders, and prepares to build a temple for the Ark of the Covenant which he brings to his new capital city, Jerusalem. He creates a center for the religion of the nation with a focus on God, and he leaves a legitimate heir to succeed him. So, just as God did not forget the anointed one, David, the psalmist prays that God will remember those who call upon God. The prayer is that God will not turn away God's face.

Second, during the funeral rites, we pray that the community will not forget the deceased. This is demonstrated through participation in the major parts of the funeral rites, namely, the vigil, the liturgy, and the committal. In order for the remembering to take place, the funeral rites need to be scheduled at times that the members of the Christian community can attend. Thus, the members will not turn away their faces on the one who was anointed as royalty, like David, in baptism, and like Jesus Christ, in death and resurrection.

In remembering the dead, we remember what God did in their lives. Whoever they were, whatever they became, the good works they did, the great words they spoke, the kind deeds they performed— all were gifts from God. In remembering the deceased, we also remember God, the source of all gifts and life. So, before deciding not to attend the funeral of a member of your Christian community, remember not to turn away your face.

Questions for Reflection: Have you ever turned away and not attended a funeral of a loved one? If yes, why? If not, why do you think people turn away?

Prayer: Mighty God, you did not forget David and his struggles to be faithful to you. In your mercy remember me, anointed in baptism as one of your children. Let your face shine on me that I might reflect your mercy to others. Praise to you, Father, Son, and Holy Spirit, for all you have done in the lives of those who have gone before me, now and for ever and ever. Amen.

Journal: How are you like David? In other words, in what ways has God not turned away but remembered you and blessed your life?

16. BLESSINGS

Scripture: (Ps 134)

> Come, bless the LORD, all you servants of the LORD,
>   who stand by night in the house of the LORD!
> Lift up your hands to the holy place
>   and bless the LORD (134:1-2).

Order of Christian Funerals: par. 15.

Reflection: I have a priest friend who, before he signs his name, closes his letters with the single word, "Blessings." "To bless" means "to wish well" or "to speak well." So, we bless God and others by wishing them the best of journeys or by speaking well of them. We can bless in the night or the day. We can bless with words or silence. We can ask God to bless us, to keep us well on our lifetime pilgrimage.

During the funeral rites for a deceased member of the Christian community, we bless the dead and the living. We bless the dead by speaking of the deeds God worked in their lives. We bless the living by our service as a reader, a musician, an usher, a pallbearer, a minister of the Eucharist. Our service is a blessing to the community. All of us are servants of the Lord, and our servant status can be demonstrated in our liturgical service in the church, the house of God.

Posture is important in blessing the living and the dead. We can trace the sign of the cross on the forehead of the dead, just like we do on ourselves with water upon entering the church. We can raise our hands upward in prayer or hold them extended over those we intend to bless. Laying our hands on the head of a person is a good posture for blessing. Greeting another in an embrace of peace is a posture of blessing. Blessing can be done while standing and touching the coffin or with a bowed head near a grave. In other words, our actions can be a sign of blessing.

God never ceases to bless us. We can do no less than wish the same wellness on the living and the dead. By remembering the blessings God has given to us, we remember to share those same blessings with others.

Questions for Reflection: In what ways can you or do you already bless the living and the dead? Who has been a recipient of your blessing? How have you received blessings?

Prayer: Redeeming God, maker of heaven and earth, I lift up my hands in blessing to you even as I ask for your blessings for me. Inspire me to speak well of all people, both living and dead. Make me a good servant. Guide me to your eternal dwelling place. I ask this through Jesus Christ the Lord. Amen.

Journal: Remember a recent funeral for a member of your family. How did he or she bless the living and the dead? How did he or she bless God? How might you make his or her blessings your own?

PART IV

Office for the Dead

The vigil for the deceased may be celebrated in the form of some part of the office for the dead. To encourage this form of the vigil, the chief hours, "Morning Prayer" and "Evening Prayer," are provided [in the *Order of Christian Funerals*].

—*Order of Christian Funerals,* par. 348.

17. Morning Prayer

Order of Christian Funerals: par. 350.

FIRST PSALM: SORROW AND HOPE

Scripture: (Ps 51)

> Have mercy on me, O God,
>   according to your steadfast love;
> according to your abundant mercy
>   blot out my transgressions.
> Wash me thoroughly from my iniquity,
>   and cleanse me from my sin.
>
> . . . .
>
> O Lord, open my lips,
>   and my mouth will declare your praise (51:1-2, 15).

Order of Christian Funerals: par. 355.

Reflection: One emotion that emerges at the time of the death of a family member or a friend is sorrow. We feel sad because a person we loved has died. We may feel lost and wander around with no sense of direction. Even though we may be surrounded by a crowd of people, we discover that we are alone. If it goes unchecked, sorrow can turn into despair.

While some sorrow is natural at the time of the death of a relative or friend, in the usual process of living it is overcome by hope. We hope that the life experienced on this side of the grave by the deceased is turned into the fullness of life on the other side of the grave. We hope that our experience of grief will be transformed by our hope in the redemption won by Jesus Christ.

The petition for mercy recognizes that God is in charge of all life. The assembly asks God to remember that only God can forgive transgressions or sins. God washes them away, like a spring shower carries away the dust and debris of the winter. In fact, God is always washing away our weaknesses and saving us. In baptism God bathed us in the streams of new life. At the time of death, we recall that first of many washings and request a final cleansing from iniquity for the deceased.

Recognizing that only God, who is greater than human goodness or sinfulness, can make us clean, we acknowledge our dependency and petition that we might offer the best words of praise. God opens lips to speak, God opens mouths to sing, and God opens the hearts of the sorrowing to give them hope. We declare these deeds of God.

Questions for Reflection: What sorrows in your life have been replaced by hope? Make a list of the sorrows and the type of hope that God gave you in the midst of each.

Prayer: Merciful God, your love is everlasting and without limit. Through the waters of baptism, you have washed away my sin. Throughout my life, you have cleansed me of my iniquities. Open my lips to praise your greatness. Turn my sorrow into the hope of seeing you face to face. I ask this through Christ the Lord. Amen.

Journal: What are the major events of cleansing that have taken place in your life? From what were you washed? How do these cleansings help you understand that God washes away our sin from birth to death?

CANTICLE: LIVING THANKS

Scripture: (Isa 38:10-14, 17-20)

> I said: In the noontide of my days
>   I must depart;
> I am consigned to the gates of Sheol
>   for the rest of my years.
> I said, I shall not see the LORD
>   in the land of the living;
> I shall look upon mortals no more
>   among the inhabitants of the world.
>
> . . . .
>
> For Sheol cannot thank you,
>   death cannot praise you;
> those who go down to the Pit cannot hope
>   for your faithfulness.
> The living, the living, they thank you,
>   as I do this day
>
> . . . .
>
> The LORD will save me,
>   and we will sing to stringed instruments
> all the days of our lives
>   at the house of the LORD (38:10-11, 18-19a, 20).

Order of Christian Funerals: par. 349.

Reflection: In the biblical world, the universe was understood to consist of three stories or three levels. Above the dome of the earth, the first level, was the dwelling place of God. The earth, shaped like a plate with mountains all around and pillars supporting it underneath, the second level, was where people lived. Under the earth, called Sheol, level three, was the dwelling place for the dead. Before Christianity transformed Sheol into hell, all of the earth was a place for the living: God lived above, people lived in the middle, and the dead lived below.

The prayer of Hezekiah, King of Judah, found in the Book of the prophet Isaiah, presupposes a three-storied universe. In the midst of his sickness, the king thinks that he will die and go to live with the rest of the dead in Sheol. He will no longer be able to worship God in the temple on earth, and he will no longer see the people who live on the earth. However, when the king recovers from his sickness, he turns his prayer into praise of God for healing him. The living give thanks, he says, and his proper response is to sing God's praises to the accompaniment of musical instruments in the Lord's house.

When the Christian community gathers together to pray, it offers living thanks to God. Especially at the time of the death of a family member or a friend, the assembly praises the God of all life. Even though the deceased was not rescued from illness, he or she was rescued from Sheol by God. The death and resurrection of Jesus burst open the gates of Sheol, the place where the dead lived, and made it possible for them to enter into heaven, where God lives. Christ's victory over death removed the barriers of the three-storied universe, uniting the level above, the level below, and the middle into one. Thus, both those alive and those who are dead offer living thanks to God.

Questions for Reflection: How do you conceive of the universe? If it helps, draw a picture of it. How does your conception of the universe affect your understanding of God, life, and death?

Prayer: Living God, through the death and resurrection of your Son, our Lord Jesus Christ, you have united all of the universe into one chorus of living thanks. Fill me with gratefulness for your gift of salvation. May I praise you all my days. Hear me through Jesus Christ, who lives with you in the unity of the Holy Spirit, for ever and ever. Amen.

Journal: Compose your own prayer of thanksgiving to God for the times you have been sick and were healed. How do your experiences of being sick and healed support your faith in the healing resurrection that awaits you on the other side of the grave?

SECOND PSALM: A. PRAISE THE LORD!

Scripture: (Ps 146)

> Praise the LORD!
> Praise the LORD, O my soul!
> I will praise the LORD as long as I live;
>   I will sing praises to my God all my life long.
> Do not put your trust in princes,
>   in mortals, in whom there is no help.
> When their breath departs, they return to the earth;
>   on that very day their plans perish (146:1-4).

Order of Christian Funerals: par. 355.

Reflection: When it comes right down to it, we must admit that only God can sustain life. We can be tricked into thinking that we sustain our own lives through exercise, eating foods high in fiber, and carefully moderating our intake of alcoholic beverages and not smoking. By taking vitamins or drinking a liquid full of nutrients, we may believe that we bolster our lives.

However, no matter whether we come to realize it early in our years or later in them, God sustains life. All things return to the earth: the leaves fall from the trees and become compost; the grass browns and decays; in the fall, the tomatoes, pumpkins, and potatoes rot in forgotten summer gardens. All people return to the earth: the bodies of kings and queens, presidents and prime ministers, rich and poor are buried, cremated, or committed to the deeps of the ocean. Only the memories of the living remain, and they too will be lost when the last one who remembers finally dies.

Beyond this life's breath, there is only God and our trust in God. That is why we sing or pray our praise of God when a family member or a friend dies. We know there is nothing we can do to sustain life, no matter how hard we try. There comes a point when the most advanced medical techniques cannot heal, when tissue replacements will do no good, when this life comes to its final end. Our trust is not placed in human beings, who cannot sustain life, but in God, who is the author of eternal life.

Jesus is our example. As a human being, he died, knowing that not even he could sustain his own life. He trusted that God would maintain his life beyond the tomb. And God did. God raised Jesus from the dead. We praise the God who brings life from death, not only for the resurrection of Jesus, but for any human being who trusts that what God did for Jesus God will do for us.

Questions for Reflection: In what ways do you attempt to sustain your life? For each way identify how it is futile. In what ways has God sustained you throughout your life?

Prayer: All praise to you, ever-living God. I praise you with the words of my lips and the songs of my heart. You are the source of all life and its sustainer. Give me a generous share of your Holy Spirit. Breathe into me your gift of eternal life. I place my trust in you, who raised your Son, Jesus Christ, from the dead. He is Lord for ever and ever. Amen.

Journal: Make a list of the members of your family and friends who have died. Identify how each trusted in God to sustain his or her life. Praise God for each person's life.

SECOND PSALM: B. DESTINY

Scripture: (Ps 150)

> Praise the LORD!
> Praise God in his sanctuary;
> praise him in his mighty firmament!
>
> . . . .
> Let everything that breathes praise the LORD!
> Praise the LORD! (150:1, 6).

Order of Christian Funerals: par. 355.

Reflection: Because we cannot know what is on the other side of death, we employ metaphors on this side to talk about what is on the other side. We use images of life now to compare what life might be like after death. Because we experience falling asleep every night and waking up the next morning, we declare that death is like falling asleep and that we will wake up in the life beyond death. Notice, however, that the metaphor "falling asleep and waking up" tells us nothing about what is on the other side of the grave.

Our faith tells us that we are destined to share in the liturgy of heaven. The metaphor here is the assembly gathered together in worship through prayer and song. Just as we praise God in this life, so we will praise God eternally in the liturgy of heaven. Likewise, the experience of shedding tears when a loved one dies will be reversed in the life beyond the grave. We will no longer cry. The victory

Jesus won over death will be shared with us in its fullness because God will do for us what God did for Jesus—raise us from the dead.

The psalms of praise, such as Psalm 150, employ images of how we extol God in this life as metaphors of how we will laud God in eternal life. It is our destiny to praise God for everything everywhere with everything at every time. All that breathes in this life is destined to breathe in the life to come. For God's greatness, we praise God.

Questions for Reflection: What is your favorite metaphor for death? What is your favorite metaphor for the next life? How do these images support your faith?

Prayer: God of all creation, everything that breathes praises you. Your mighty deed of raising Jesus from the dead demonstrates your surpassing greatness. Grant me the grace to offer you fitting worship and praise. Guide me through this life to share in the victory of eternal life with the Lord Jesus Christ, who lives and reigns with you and the Holy Spirit, one God, for ever and ever. Amen.

Journal: Recall the lives of two or three deceased family members or friends. Identify what each's favorite metaphor for death was and what each's favorite metaphor for eternal life was. How did their metaphors illustrate their faith?

READING: SPIRITUAL BOND

Scripture: (1 Thess 4:14) . . . [S]ince we believe that Jesus died and rose again, even so, through Jesus, God will bring with him those who have died (4:14).

Order of Christian Funerals: par. 349.

Reflection: The Liturgy of the Hours is the official prayer of the whole church throughout the day. It consists of singing psalms, voicing prayers of praise and petition, and listening to the words of Scripture at various times of the day, primarily morning and evening. In the morning, as the sun rises, we remember the resurrection of Jesus. In the evening, as the sun sets and the lights of night are lighted, we remember that the brightness of the resurrection has conquered the darkness of death.

The community's celebration of the hours serves to unite the whole day from dawn to dusk. In monasteries, where not only morning prayer and evening prayer are celebrated, but the additional hours of readings, midday prayer, and night prayer are a part of the community's daily routine, the day is further bound together in one grand chorus of praise and thanks to God. The praying of the hours serves to remind the community that the spiritual bond that unites the living and the dead cannot be broken.

The Liturgy of the Hours is like a pole linking heaven and earth. Just like a man and woman join themselves together in wedded love, so the Church, through Christ, is married to heaven in a spiritual bond. Thus, the living pray to God for the deceased, and the dead, who live with God eternally, pray for the living. We pray that God will remove all imperfections from those who have died so that they may be made worthy to see the face of God. We ask those who have died to pray that God will guide the steps of our journey for the duration of this life, through death, and into eternal life.

It is appropriate that we demonstrate the spiritual bond that unites the whole Church through the praying of the hours at the time of the death of a loved one. Instead of a vigil celebration, Evening Prayer for the dead may be celebrated. Before the procession from the mortuary to the church for the funeral liturgy, Morning Prayer can be celebrated. If the funeral liturgy is held in the evening with final disposition the next day, Morning Prayer could be prayed before the procession to the place of committal. The bond of prayer strengthens all, both the living and the dead.

Questions for Reflection: How do you understand the spiritual bond that exists between the living and the dead in the Church? How do you experience this spiritual bond?

Prayer: God of the living and the dead, your Son, Jesus, died and rose again as the promise of my resurrection from the dead. Through the prayer and praise of your Church, bind me more closely to both those on earth and in heaven. Hear my prayer through the Lord Jesus Christ, who lives and reigns with you and the Holy Spirit, one God, for ever and ever. Amen.

Journal: Have you had any experience of praying the Liturgy of the Hours? If you have, how did it serve to unite the day? How did it remind you of your unity with the Church in heaven? If you haven't had any experience praying the Liturgy of the Hours, what measures can you take to stop in the morning and evening to offer some type of prayer of praise and thanksgiving?

CANTICLE OF ZECHARIAH: BREAKING DAWN

Scripture: (Luke 1:68-79) . . . Zechariah was filled with the Holy Spirit and spoke this prophecy:

"By the tender mercy of our God,
    the dawn from on high will break upon us,
to give light to those who sit in darkness and in the shadow of
    death,
    to guide our feet into the way of peace" (1:67, 78-79).

Order of Christian Funerals: par. 350.

Reflection: For many people, dawn is their favorite time of the day. They stand in front of the window or sit in a chair where the first streaks of the light can be seen shattering the darkness of the eastern horizon. In the mountains, by hours the light of the day precedes the sun, which seems to suddenly pop over the granite hills. On the ocean, the dawn lights up the water, streaking it with shades of orange and red.

The stories about Christ's resurrection center on the discovery of the empty tomb at dawn. The announcement of the light of a new day with the sun rising corresponds to the proclamation that God raised Jesus from the dead and began a new age of eternal life for humanity. The light of the darkness of the finality of death has been shattered forever by the power of Christ's resurrection from the dead. He has made life an eternal day.

When we gather in the morning to pray for the deceased before the procession to the church for the funeral liturgy or, if the funeral liturgy was held the previous evening, before the procession to the place of final disposition, we remember God's promise. Out of God's mercy, the dawn breaks upon us. Out of God's mercy, the resurrection of Christ gives light to the dead and guides them to the place of eternal peace. The dawn reminds us of God's gift of eternal light and life.

Questions for Reflection: In what ways for you is the dawn a herald of a new day, a new life, a new beginning? In what ways for you is the dawn a herald of the resurrection of Christ and of eternal life?

Prayer: Merciful God, you created the sun to give me light during the day. Every morning it breaks the darkness and bathes the earth in newness. You raised your Son, Jesus Christ, from the dead and conquered the shadows of death. Every morning I recall his new life which gives me hope. Guide my feet in the ways of your peace to the eternal life and light you promise. I ask this through Jesus Christ the Lord. Amen.

Journal: Get up early enough to watch the sunrise tomorrow. As the dawn breaks, describe what you see. Go outside and describe what you taste, smell, hear, and feel. How does the dawn help you understand resurrection?

18. Evening Prayer

Order of Christian Funerals: par. 351.

FIRST PSALM: KEEPER OF LIFE

Scripture: (Ps 121)

I lift up my eyes to the hills—
    from where will my help come?
My help comes from the LORD,
    who made heaven and earth.

. . . .

The LORD is your keeper;
    the LORD is your shade at your right hand.

. . . .

    [The LORD] will keep your life.
The LORD will keep
    your going out and your coming in
    from this time on and forevermore (121:1-2, 5, 7b-8).

Order of Christian Funerals: par. 349.

Reflection: Like King Arthur's Knights of the Round Table and their quest for the Holy Grail, some people speak about searching for God. Their exploration takes them to mountain peaks and ocean depths, to churches and synagogues and mosques, to conventions and gatherings. However, we can become so focused on the quest that we miss the God who is looking for us. It is not God who needs to be found by us. We need to be discovered by God.

The psalmist emphasized that point in a song written for pilgrims beginning their ascent to Jerusalem and its Temple. Looking up to Mount Zion, where God lived, the people knew from where their help came. God had found Abraham and brought him to a new land. God had found Moses and commissioned him to lead Israel out of Egypt to the land flowing with milk and honey. Countless times God found people and fed, watered, and rescued them. Help came from the Creator of heaven and earth. God, it seems, was always in the process of finding lost people.

God also keeps life. In the past, God kept the lives of the chosen people close to God's heart. No matter whether they were going from freedom to slavery or from slavery to freedom, from victory in war or to defeat in battle, from going up to Jerusalem or returning home from the holy city, God kept their lives. Demonstrating how much God desires to find people and to keep their lives, God raised Jesus from the dead. God kept the life of Christ to show us the eternal life awaiting us.

When we gather, Christ, the Mediator and High Priest, assures us of life. Through the assembly's prayer and song, the Spirit fills us with divine life. In the midst of the death of a family member or a friend, we proclaim eternal life. The keeper of all life searches for us in order to find us and give us everlasting life. If we aren't too busy on our own quest, we can be found by God.

Questions for Reflection: When has God found you? How was your life kept? How has God been your help? Make a list of the ways.

Prayer: Creator of heaven and earth, keeper of all life, you never cease to search for me. Keep me from being so preoccupied with my own quest that I fail to recognize you when you find me. Keep my life through the Holy Spirit. Grant me the gift of eternal life through Jesus Christ, your Son. Eternal God, guard my going and coming now and for ever. Amen.

Journal: Recall a member of your family or a friend who has died. How did God find that person? How did God keep the life of that person?

SECOND PSALM: INTERCESSOR

Scripture: (Ps 130)

> Lord, hear my voice!
> Let your ears be attentive
> to the voice of my supplications!
>
> . . . .
>
> I wait for the LORD, my soul waits,
> and in his word I hope;
> my soul waits for the Lord
> more than those who watch for the morning
>
> . . . .

O Israel, hope in the LORD!
For with the LORD there is steadfast love,
and with him is great power to redeem (130:2, 5-6b, 7).

Order of Christian Funerals: par. 355.

Reflection: The person who intercedes is one who intervenes between two others. He or she intervenes in the hope of bringing the two people closer together. We proclaim Christ to be our intercessor with God because he was fully human and is fully divine. No one is better able than Christ to bring our needs to God's attention.

We make our various supplications into one when we pray the psalms. We join our voices to that of the inspired-by-God writer of the song, and being the body of Christ, we pray in the voice of Christ and ask God to grant our petitions. Of course, God already knows what we need, but because of our human limitations we express our dependency upon God through the very psalms God inspired us to sing.

Once we have brought our prayers in Christ to God, we wait for God to act. The praying of the psalm is an act of placing our hope in God's word. The One who inspires us to ask for what we need gives us the very words to use to make our requests. Our hope is as strong and confident as the person on watch.

In the days when cities had walls, when outposts had stockades and camps needed protection from enemies, a watch was stationed. The person on watch walked along the top of the walls to be sure that no one crawled over them and entered the sleeping city. Outposts had raised platforms at each corner to guard the stockade from enemy attack. In order to keep someone from entering a camp, a sentinel was posted. That person's job was to protect those who were asleep and to awaken them if danger approached. When morning arrived, the watch was over.

The morning of God's power was demonstrated by the redeeming act of Jesus. God showed us how strong our hope needs to be through the suffering and death of Christ, who did not give up hope that God would raise him from the dead. God's steadfast love redeemed the whole world. During the night of Jesus' death, God kept watch and raised him to eternal life.

Jesus, our intercessor, brings this life to us even as he brings our prayer to God. When we face the death of a family member or a friend, we pray that God will keep watch and strengthen us as we keep watch for the morning of new life. It is a petition that God grants through Christ.

Questions for Reflection: Who has served as an intercessor in your family, work, play? What did he or she do? What were the results of his or her intervention?

Prayer: Steadfast God, let your ears hear my prayers. I hope in your word of promise and I trust your constant love. Send your Holy Spirit to help me keep watch throughout my life for the morning of eternal life. Redeem me through the suffering, death, and resurrection of the Lord Jesus Christ, who lives and reigns with you and the Holy Spirit, one God, for ever and ever. Amen.

Journal: On what occasions have you placed your hope in God's word? How did you wait for God to act? In what ways were you like a watch waiting for the morning?

CANTICLE: THREE LEVELS OF LIFE

Scripture: (Phil 2:6-11)

> [Jesus,] though he was in the form of God,
>> did not regard equality with God
>> as something to be exploited,
> but emptied himself,
>> taking the form of a slave,
>> being born in human likeness.
> And being found in human form,
>> he humbled himself
> and became obedient to the point of death—
>> even death on a cross.
> Therefore God also highly exalted him
>> and gave him the name
>> that is above every name,
> so that at the name of Jesus
>> every knee should bend,
>> in heaven and on earth and under the earth,
> and every tongue should confess
>> that Jesus Christ is Lord,
>> to the glory of God the Father (2:6-11).

Order of Christian Funerals: par. 360.

Reflection: When the Scriptures were written, the general population thought of their world as consisting of three levels, like a three-floored skyscraper: above, middle, below. The first story of the universe was above, the place over the dome of the sky where God lived. The middle level, conceived of as a plate with supporting pillars and mountains to keep inhabitants from falling off, was made for people. Below or under the plate was where the dead lived. For people who had not heard of galaxies and solar systems, each of the three floors of their world contained life.

The passage from Paul's letter to the Philippians presupposes the three-storied universe. Quoting an early Christian hymn, Paul portrays Jesus as coming from the world above, where he was in the form of God, to the world in the middle, where he was born in the form of a human being, and having died on a cross, entering the world below. Because of his obedience, Jesus was not left in the world below, but raised to the world above. As the exalted Lord, he is worshiped by those who live above, in the middle, and below the earth. All of life bends its knee before Jesus Christ the Lord.

The paschal mystery, God's presence revealed through Jesus' suffering, death, and resurrection, shows us life at every level of the universe. More accurately, the paschal mystery unites the three-storied world into one harmonious whole through which flows divine life. From the level above, God pours out eternal life on all of creation. In the middle level, we receive God's life, which permeates and fills all with hope. Passing through death, we discover not the end, but more life. What Jesus revealed is that no person and no thing ever disappears. Like Jesus who changed his form as he passed from one level of the universe to another, we are changed by God as we move from one level to another.

When we face the death of a family member or a friend, we can find comfort in the three levels of life revealed by God through the paschal mystery of Jesus Christ. We can find hope that as we pass from one level to another, all of us will one day be gathered together in God's kingdom, a level of life which has not yet been fully revealed to us.

Questions for Reflection: How do you think of the universe? Where do you locate the divinity, yourself, the dead, the reign of God? How do you understand the paschal mystery?

Prayer: God above all, your Son, Jesus Christ, did not exploit his divinity, but emptied himself and became human, coming to live in the middle of our world and revealing the paschal mystery through his suffering and death. You did not allow the world of the dead to have any power over him, but by raising him to life, you revealed the glory of your reign to come, where I hope to share your life and confess that Jesus Christ is Lord for ever and ever. Amen.

Journal: Using your answers to the questions for reflection, draw a picture of the universe as you suppose it to be. Based on your drawing, how would you rewrite the passage from Philippians to reflect your universe? In other words, today how would you portray God as revealing eternal life pervading and uniting the universe?

READING: NO VICTORY, NO STING

Scripture: (1 Cor 15:55-57)

"Where, O death, is your victory?
Where, O death, is your sting?"
The sting of death is sin, and the power of sin is the law. But thanks be to God, who gives us the victory through our Lord Jesus Christ (15:55-57).

Order of Christian Funerals: par. 368.

Reflection: When we look down into a coffin and stare at the face of the deceased person lying there, we are stung by death's finality. Death is cold, hard, and lifeless. The eyes no longer see, the lungs no longer breathe, the heart has ceased to pump, rigor mortis has overcome even the largest of muscles. In its appearance, death looks like it has claimed another victim. Death is victorious again.

However, what we see is not always reality. In fact, we don't see reality as it exists; we see reality as we are. Because we are human and experience the death of all humankind—not to mention everything else in the world—we can conclude that death is final, the end. However, there is more to reality than what we see or experience. Death does not deal us a lethal blow; it is merely the result of being a sinful human being. The example of the Lord Jesus Christ assures us that death has no power over us. Just as God raised Christ from the dead, we too are promised eternal life. Death looks final, but it fails to disclose the reality of the victory won by Christ.

By praying the Liturgy of the Hours, especially Morning Prayer and Evening Prayer, we celebrate Christ's victorious defeat of death and its sting. In the morning, we recall Christ's resurrection—his defeat of death's sting. In the evening, we remember the gifts of the day and give thanks to God for the paschal mystery—Christ's passover through death to life—our hope.

Through the rhythmic praying of the psalms, we join our voices to those present and the whole Church, forming a chorus of intercession for the deceased and demonstrating our concern and support for the family members and friends of the loved one. Through the Scriptures and prayers, we become a sign of faith and hope in the paschal mystery. We profess that death can no longer affect us. What God did for Jesus, God promises to do for us. Instead of seeing finality when we look into the coffin, we see abundant life.

Questions for Reflection: In what ways have you experienced the victory of Christ over death when attending a funeral? How did your own faith and hope in the paschal mystery—the death and resurrection of Christ—help you to show concern and support for the family and friends of the deceased?

Prayer: God of life, when it looked like death had defeated your Son, Jesus Christ, you made him victorious by raising him to new life. No longer does death have the last word. Strengthen my faith and encourage my hope in the face of death so that I may show my concern and offer support to others dealing with the death of a loved one. On the day of my death, let me share the victory of the Lord Jesus Christ, who lives and reigns with you and the Holy Spirit, one God, for ever and ever. Amen.

Journal: When have you perceived reality to be one way and discovered it to be different? What was that experience? What did you learn from it? How did it change you?

CANTICLE OF MARY: PROMISE KEPT

Scripture: (Luke 1:46-55) . . . Mary said,

> "My soul magnifies the Lord,
>   and my spirit rejoices in God my Savior. . . .
> . . . .
> His mercy is for those who fear him
>   from generation to generation.
> He has shown strength with his arm;
>   he has scattered the proud in the thoughts of their hearts.
> He has brought down the powerful from their thrones,
>   and lifted up the lowly;
> he has filled the hungry with good things,
>   and sent the rich away empty.
> He has helped his servant Israel,
>   in remembrance of his mercy,
> according to the promise he made to our ancestors. . ."
>   (1:46-47, 50-55a).

Order of Christian Funerals: par. 351.

Reflection: In a world in which promises are as fragile as crystal goblets sent through the mail in a box with no packing material to cushion them, there is only One whose promise is always kept—God. Besides serving as an outline for the rest of Luke's Gospel, the song of praise attributed to Mary declares that through Jesus, God kept the promise made to people of the past. It was not because God had to keep the promise of redemption; it was because God is rich in mercy toward people.

Through his simple words of wisdom and parables, Jesus scattered those whose pride was found in worldly hearts and revealed God's kingdom to the lowly peasants. Those who sat on thrones ruling others discovered that the real throne was the cross and serving others was more powerful than exercising authority over them. Those who hungered were fed, not only with bread and fish, but with the body and blood of Christ. The rich went their own way, discovering that their wealth meant nothing in the new world.

The whole people, Israel, from which was born a new people, Christianity, was remembered by God, who kept the promise made to them. Such a promise kept is worthy of remembrance when we are dealing with the death of a family member or a friend. In a world of broken promises, we find unwavering hope in God's promise of redemption which Jesus brought about through his own life, death, and resurrection. What God did in the past, God continues in the present. God keeps the promise from one generation to the next. Our security in God's promise enables us to praise God for the gift of the life of the dead person, who has passed through death to the joy-giving life of eternity.

Questions for Reflection: What promises made to you by others have recently been broken? What promises have you made to others and broken? How do broken promises affect your trust in God's promise?

Prayer: God my Savior, I praise you for the mercy you have shown to me and my ancestors. Scatter my proud thoughts and never permit me to exploit power I might have over others. Satisfy my hunger with your word and make me rich in understanding. Keep your promise of redemption through Jesus Christ, your Son, who lives and reigns with you and the Holy Spirit, one God, for ever and ever. Amen.

Journal: Make a list of what you think are God's promises and how they were kept. What promises has God made to you and kept? How does God's promise-keeping give you hope beyond the grave?

Planning Funeral Rites

Whenever possible, ministers should involve the family in planning the funeral rites: in the choice of texts and rites provided in the ritual, in the selection of music for the rites, and in the designation of liturgical ministers.

Planning of the funeral rites may take place during the visit of the pastor or other minister at some appropriate time after the death and before the vigil service. Ministers should explain to the family the meaning and significance of each of the funeral rites, especially the vigil, the funeral liturgy, and the rite of committal.

—*Order of Christian Funerals,* par. 17.

1. Vigil for the Deceased

Vigil for the Deceased

INTRODUCTORY RITES

Greeting (no. 69):   A   B   C   D

Opening Song (no. 70):_____

Invitation to prayer (no. 71)

Opening Prayer (no. 72):

   A   B   or no. chosen from nos. 398–399_____

LITURGY OF THE WORD

First Reading: No. 74 or no. chosen from Part III _____

Responsorial Psalm: No. 75 or no. chosen from Part III _____

Gospel: No. 76 or no. chosen from Part III _____

Homily (no. 77)

PRAYER OF INTERCESSION

Litany (no. 78)

The Lord's Prayer (no. 79):   A   B   C

Concluding Prayer (no. 80):

   A   B   or no. chosen from nos. 398–399 _____

CONCLUDING RITE

Blessing (no. 81):   A   B

MINISTERS

Bishop/Priest/Deacon/Leader _____

Reader _____

Homilist _____

Song Leader/Cantor _____

Musicians _____

Vigil for the Deceased with Reception at the Church

INTRODUCTORY RITES

Greeting (no. 82):   A   B   C   D

Sprinkling with Holy Water (no. 83)

[Placing of the Pall] (no. 84)

Entrance Procession (Song) (no. 85):_____

[Placing of Christian Symbols] (no. 86)

Invitation to Prayer (no. 87)

Opening Prayer (no. 88):

   A   B   or no. chosen from nos. 398–399 _____

LITURGY OF THE WORD

First Reading: No. 90 or no. chosen from Part III _____

Responsorial Psalm: No. 91 or no. chosen from Part III _____

Gospel: No. 92 or no. chosen from Part III _____

Homily (no. 93)

PRAYER OF INTERCESSION

Litany (no. 94)

The Lord's Prayer (no. 95):   A   B   C

Concluding Prayer (no. 96):

   A   B   or no. chosen from nos. 398–399 _____

CONCLUDING RITE

Blessing (no. 97):   A   B

Bishop/Priest/Deacon/Leader _____

Reader _____

Homilist _____

Song Leader/Cantor _____

Musicians _____

Servers/Assistants _____

Pall Bearers _____

Pall Placers _____

Christian Symbol Placers _____

2. Related Rites and Prayers

Prayers after Death

Invitation to Prayer (no. 104):   A   B

Reading (no. 105):   A   B   C   or no. chosen from Part III _____

The Lord's Prayer (no. 106):   A   B

Concluding Prayers:

    For the deceased person: No. 107 or no. 398

    For the mourners: No. 107 or no. 399

Blessing (no. 108):   A   B

Bishop/Priest/Deacon/Leader _____

Reader _____

Gathering in the Presence of the Body

Sign of the Cross (no. 112)

Scripture Verse (no. 113):   A   B

Sprinkling with Holy Water (no. 114): A B C

Psalm (no. 115): A B or no. in Part III _____

The Lord's Prayer (no. 116): A B

Concluding Prayer (no. 117):

A B or no. chosen from nos. 398–399 _____

Blessing (no. 118): A B

MINISTERS

Bishop/Priest/Deacon/Leader _____

Reader _____

Transfer of the Body to the Church or to the Place of Committal

Invitation (no. 121)

Scripture Verse (no. 122): A B

Litany (no. 123)

The Lord's Prayer (no. 124)

Concluding Prayer (no. 125):

A B C or no. chosen from nos. 398–399 _____

Invitation to the Procession (no. 126)

Procession to the Church or to the Place of Committal: No. 127

or no. chosen from Part III, 16: Antiphons and Psalms _____

or Song: _____

MINISTERS

Bishop/Priest/Deacon/Leader _____

Reader _____

Song Leader/Cantor _____

Musicians _____

Pall Bearers _____

3. Funeral Mass

Greeting (no. 159):   A   B   C   D

Sprinkling with Holy Water (no. 160)

[Placing of the Pall] (no. 161)

Entrance Procession (Song) (no. 162): _____

[Placing of Christian Symbols] (no. 163)

Opening Prayer (no. 164):

   A   B   C   D   or no. chosen from no. 398 _____

LITURGY OF THE WORD

Readings

   Old Testament Reading: No. chosen from Part III _____

   Responsorial Psalm: No. chosen from Part III _____

   New Testament Reading:

     No. chosen from Part III _____

   Alleluia Verses and Verses Before the Gospel:

     No. chosen from Part III _____

   Gospel: No. chosen from Part III _____

Homily (no. 166)

General Intercessions (no. 167):

   A   B   or no. chosen from no. 401 _____

LITURGY OF THE EUCHARIST

Hymn During the Preparation of the Gifts: _____

Communion Hymn: _____

FINAL COMMENDATION

Invitation to Prayer (no. 171):

   A   B   or no. chosen from no. 402 _____

Silence (no. 172)

[Signs of Farewell] (no. 173)

Song of Farewell (no. 174) or Other Song _____

Prayer of Commendation (no. 175):   A   B

PROCESSION TO THE PLACE OF COMMITTAL

(no. 176):   A   B   C   D

MINISTERS

Bishop/Priest/Deacon/Leader _____

Readers _____

Homilist _____

Song Leader/Cantor _____

Musicians _____

Pall Bearers _____

Pall Placers _____

Servers/Assistants _____

Christian Symbol Placers _____

Eucharistic Ministers _____

Gift Bearers _____

4. Funeral Liturgy Outside Mass

INTRODUCTORY RITES

Greeting (no. 184):   A   B   C   D

Sprinkling with Holy Water (no. 185)

[Placing of the Pall] (no. 186)

Entrance Procession (Song) (no. 187): _____

[Placing of Christian Symbols] (no. 188)

Invitation to Prayer (no. 189)

Opening Prayer (no. 190):

   A   B   C   D   or no. chosen from no. 398 _____

LITURGY OF THE WORD

Readings

   Old Testament Reading: No. chosen from Part III _____

   Responsorial Psalm: No. chosen from Part III _____

   New Testament Reading: No. chosen from Part III _____

   Alleluia Verses and Verses Before the Gospel:

   No. chosen from Part III _____

   Gospel: No. chosen from Part III _____

Homily (no. 192)

General Intercessions (no. 193):

   A   B   or no. chosen from no. 401 _____

The Lord's Prayer (no. 194):   A   B

FINAL COMMENDATION

Invitation to Prayer (no. 198):

   A   B   or no. chosen from no. 402 _____

Silence (no. 199)

[Signs of Farewell] (no. 200)

Song of Farewell (no. 201) or Other Song _____

Prayer of Commendation (no. 202):   A   B

PROCESSION TO THE PLACE OF COMMITTAL

(no. 203):   A   B   C   D

MINISTERS

Bishop/Priest/Deacon/Leader _____

Readers _____

Homilist _____

Song Leader/Cantor _____

Musicians _____

Pall Bearers _____

Pall Placers _____

Servers/Assistants _____

Christian Symbol Placers _____

5. Rite of Committal

Invitation (no. 216)

Scripture Verse (no. 217):   A   B   C   D

Prayer over the Place of Committal (no. 218):   A   B   C

   or no. chosen from no. 405 _____

Committal (no. 219):   A   B   or no. chosen from no. 406 _____

Intercessions (no. 220):

   A   B   or no. chosen from no. 407 _____

The Lord's Prayer (no. 221)

Concluding Prayer (no. 222):

    A   B   or no. chosen from no. 408 _____

Prayer over the People (no. 223):   A   B

MINISTERS

Bishop/Priest/Deacon/Leader _____

Reader _____

Song Leader/Cantor _____

Musicians _____

Pall Bearers _____

Servers/Assistants _____

6. Rite of Committal with Final Commendation

Invitation (no. 224):   A   B

Scripture Verse (no. 225):   A   B   C   D

Prayer over the Place of Committal (no. 226):   A   B   C

    or no. chosen from no. 405 _____

Invitation to Prayer (no. 227):

    A   B   or no. chosen from no. 402 _____

Silence (no. 228)

[Signs of Farewell] (no. 229)

Song of Farewell (no. 230) or Other Song _____

Prayer of Commendation (no. 231):   A   B

Committal (no. 232)

Prayer over the People (no. 233):   A   B

MINISTERS

Bishop/Priest/Deacon/Leader _____

Reader _____

Song Leader/Cantor _____

Musicians _____

Pall Bearers _____

Servers/Assistants _____

17. Morning Prayer

Introductory Verse (no. 374)

Hymn (no. 375): _____

Psalmody (no. 376):

   First Psalm

   Canticle

   Second Psalm: A   B

Reading: No. 377 or no. chosen from Part III _____

Homily (no. 377)

Responsory (no. 378)

Canticle of Zechariah (no. 379)

Intercessions (no. 380)

The Lord's Prayer (no. 381)

Concluding Prayer (no. 382):

   A   B   C   or no. chosen from no. 398 _____

Dismissal (no. 383):   A   B

[Procession to the Place of Committal] (no. 384):   A   B   C   D

MINISTERS

Bishop/Priest/Deacon/Leader _____

Reader _____

Homilist _____

Song Leader/Cantor _____

Musicians _____

Pall Bearers _____

Servers/Assistants _____

18. Evening Prayer

Introductory Verse (no. 386)

Hymn (no. 387): _____

Psalmody (no. 388):

   First Psalm

   Second Psalm

   Canticle

Reading: No. 389 or no. chosen from Part III _____

Homily (no. 389)

Responsory (no. 390):   A   B

Canticle of Mary (no. 391)

Intercessions (no. 392)

The Lord's Prayer (no. 393)

Concluding Prayer (no. 394):

   A   B   C   or no. chosen from no. 398 _____

Dismissal (no. 395):   A   B

MINISTERS

Bishop/Priest/Deacon/Leader _____

Reader _____

Homilist _____

Song Leader/Cantor _____

Musicians _____

Servers/Assistants _____

Annotated List
of Scripture Texts for
13. Funerals for Adults

2 Maccabees 12:43-46
   It is good and holy to think of the dead rising again.

Job 19:1, 23-27
   I know that my Redeemer lives.

Psalms

23

   The Lord is my shepherd; there is nothing I shall want.

25

   All my hope is in the Lord.

27

   The Lord is my light and my salvation.

42 & 43

   My soul is thirsting for the living God: when shall I see him
   face to face?

63

   My soul is thirsting for you, O Lord my God.

103

   The Lord is kind and merciful, full of compassion and pity.

116

   Precious in the eyes of the Lord is the death of the faithful.

122

   I rejoiced when I heard them say: Let us go to the house of the
   Lord.

130

Out of the depths I cry to you, Lord; let your ears be attentive.

143

O Lord, hear my prayer and guide me with your Spirit.

Wisdom

3:1-9 or 3:1-6, 9

The souls of the just are in the hand of God.

4:7-15

Even though the just die early, they are at rest.

Isaiah 25:6a, 7-9

The Lord will destroy death for ever.

Lamentations 3:17-26

It is good to wait in silence for the Lord God to save.

Daniel 12:1-3

Many of those who sleep in the dust of the earth shall awake.

Matthew

5:1-12a

Rejoice and be glad for your reward will be great in heaven.

11:25-30

Jesus says, Come to me and I will give you rest.

25:1-13

When the bridegroom comes, go out to meet him.

25:31-46

Come, you whom my Father has blessed.

Mark 15:33-39; 16:1-6 or 15:33-39

"My God, my God, why have you forsaken me?"

Luke

7:11-17

Young man, I say to you, arise.

12:35-40

Be prepared for the return of the master of the house.

20:35-38

He is not God of the dead, but of the living, for to him all are alive.

23:33, 39-43

Today you will be with me in paradise.

23:44-46, 50, 52-53; 24:1-6a or 23:44-46, 50, 52-53

Father, I put my life in your hands.

24:13-35 or 24:13-16, 28-35

Was it not necessary that the Christ should suffer and so enter into his glory?

John

5:24-29

Whoever hears my word and believes has passed from death to life.

6:37-40

All who believe in the Son will have eternal life and I will raise them to life again on the last day.

6:51-58

All who eat this bread will live for ever; and I will raise them up on the last day.

11:17-27 or 11:21-27

I am the resurrection and the life.

11:32-45

Lazarus, come out.

12:23-28 or 12:23-26

If a grain of wheat falls on the ground and dies, it yields a rich harvest.

14:1-6

There are many rooms in my Father's house.

17:24-26

Father, I want those you have given me to be with me where I am.

19:17-18, 25-30

Jesus bowed his head and gave up his spirit.

Acts 10:34-43 or 10:34-36, 42-43
God has appointed Jesus to judge everyone, alive and dead.

Romans

5:5-11
Having been justified by his blood, we will be saved from God's anger through him.

5:17-21
Where sin increased, there grace abounded all the more.

6:3-9 or 6:3-4, 8-9
Let us walk in newness of life.

8:14-23
We groan while we wait for the redemption of our bodies.

8:31b-35, 38-39
Who can ever come between us and the love of Christ?

14:7-9, 10b-12
Whether alive or dead, we belong to the Lord.

1 Corinthians

15:20-23, 24b-28 or 15:20-23
All people will be brought to life in Christ.

15:51-57
Death is swallowed up in victory.

2 Corinthians

4:14–5:1
What is seen is transitory; what is unseen is eternal.

5:1, 6-10
We have an everlasting home in heaven.

Philippians 3:20-21
Jesus will transfigure these lowly bodies of ours to be like his glorious body.

1 Thessalonians 4:13-18
We shall stay with the Lord for ever.

2 Timothy 2:8-13
If we have died with him, we shall live with him.

1 John

3:1-2
> We shall see God as God really is.

3:14-16
> We have passed from death to life, because we love our brothers and sisters.

Revelation

14:13
> Happy are those who die in the Lord.

20:11–21:1
> The dead have been judged according to their works.

21:1-5a, 6b-7
> There will be no more death.

Index of Scripture Texts